I Know Another Way
from Tintern to St Davids

edited by
Jon Gower

with photographs by
Paul Davies

First Impression—2002

ISBN 1 84323 126 3

The writing of this book was commissioned with help from
the Welsh Writers Trust, Academi and Chapter Arts Centre in Cardiff.

The volume is published with the support of the
Arts Council of Wales.

*Printed in Wales at
Gomer Press, Llandysul, Ceredigion SA44 4QL*

CONTENTS

EDITOR'S PREFACE

The journalist, editor and campaigner Robin Reeves knew his way. It's the path that takes you to a better country and he walked it just as surely as he did the real land, with its harsh rocks and green quilting. After he died, some of us gathered to consider ways of further developing his legacy to us, that of friendship and wisdom and that laugh of his when he was tickled pink. He'd have liked to share our rivulet of red wine and we'd have loved him to. But life is a robber and steals away the most precious things.

Robin had long nursed a dream to see a long distance path which followed the old pilgrim trails. He had walked them. He had corresponded with people about the economic contribution of such a path, seeing both a pragmatic and a spiritual dimension to the venture. As his illness grew so did his desire to realise the dream, and this book is one step in that direction – a lyrical argument, if you like, for something that would need a concord of local authorities, a lot of discrete signage and a pool of goodwill to create. He also wanted David James to contribute, on the strength of their epistolary exchange of ideas and enthusiasm for the idea. Despite his advanced years David James did write the introduction, with the help of his daughter, the storyteller Mary Medlicott, but sadly David died as the book was going to press. His was a shaping spirit behind this publication and the sadness at his passing is matched by a gladness that he was able to make his mark.

So six writers crossed south Wales, from the stone arcs of Tintern Abbey to the hidden cathedral of St Davids. This pilgrim progress happened in the winter of 2001 and the spring of 2002, each walker doing his or her segment at different times but not in series, so sometimes flowers bloom in unexpected places. At handover points you often get two perspectives on the same place – baton changes where one journey ends and another starts. All of the authors knew Robin in different degrees, and so he's present on every page, keeping step with a view of the best way to proceed.

Just as a bluebell yields some of its secrets as a microtome cuts sections thin enough to fit under the microscope slide, so too do these walked sections of Wales. Jim Perrin maps an emotional journey through south-east Wales, where social decay dishonours some of the socialist giants who hoped and worked for a better place. Robert Minhinnick follows a snaking route up the Valleys, heading for Penrhys, that byword for deprivation. He brings his poetic sensibility to an area which now spawns angry books and argues that some lyric voices might also be welcomed. Patrick Dobbs, a hill farmer, describes a countryside changed forever by foot and mouth and there is a real tone of elegy here, even though it's written by a funny man, a performance poet as well as son of the soil. I walked my home county, Carmarthenshire and found a language fleeing and one in the ascendance. Osi Rhys Osmond, a visual artist, polemicist with a mind which sherbet-fizzes with ideas, heads for Nevern from Llandysul. The last leg is left to Christine Evans, who knows a pilgrim place, as she lives on Bardsey island for part of the year.

Gracing all of the book are the photographs of Paul Adrian Davies, the New York based photographer who walked the whole route, in bleak mid-winter and signally arrived at St. Davids day on March 1st.

Singularly and severally, these words and images create a multi-faceted portrait of a Wales which clings to the old ways despite the very powerful winds of change which threaten to scour away the very rocks, or snuff out a language, or take us all with them. This band of pilgrims is challenged, seduced, angered and uplifted by Wales, from urban sprawl to mystic emptiness. As with all love affairs, this true course does not run smoothly, but it does lead, if not up the garden path, very surely to home.

Jon Gower

FOREWORD

St Davids has long been the object of pilgrimage. It is a beautiful, magical place and, as Menevia or Mynyw, it was where the sixth-century monk, Dewi Sant, founded the monastery from which he carried out his life's work and where he died. At the hour of his death, reportedly, angels filled Vallis Rosina, the valley in which the monastery was sited, with perfumed air and music.

According to Gerald the Welshman, author of the second *Life of St David*, St Davids was not only the deathplace of Dewi Sant. It had been where this simple-living preacher and teacher was born. Whether or not Gerald's information was true – he was the first person to put it in writing – it added greatly to the compelling attractions of Menevia as a worthy object of pilgrimage where people throughout the Middle Ages and afterwards could pay their respects to the memory and also, reputedly, the bones of the holy man.

During the five hundred years that elapsed between Dewi Sant's death and the emergence of the first *Life* of him composed by Rhygyfarch at the end of the eleventh century, Dewi Sant himself had been virtually forgotten. Rhygyfarch's *Life* initiated the important process of recollection and recognition that eventually gained David the status of patron saint of Wales. The work itself was a call for David, Dewi Sant, to be regarded as a leader for Wales; it was steeped in politics, for Rhygyfarch was the son of Sulien, Bishop of St Davids, at a time when the Celtic church had come under obvious threat.

In 1081 William the Conqueror had made a momentous and surprising visit to this remote centre of Christianity. His purpose in travelling so far west was undoubtedly less to do with pilgrimage than with assessing the scale of the task that remained to him in asserting Norman rule over this part of Britain. Normanisation of the Celtic church was part of the task and one of the ways it was carried out in St Davids was through the installation of Norman bishops. Another was the building by one of those bishops, Peter de Leia, of an imposing Norman cathedral where the simple Celtic monastery had been. It is no small irony that, even as the raising of it effected William the Conqueror's purpose, Peter de Leia's

cathedral, lovely in its purple stone, also ensured the continuance and growth in popular memory of the Welshness of Dewi Sant.

Nowadays people come to St Davids in droves. Many come in cars. More come in their tour buses dressed in their holiday gear. But it is appropriate that, in the future, an increasing number may perhaps arrive on foot at the end of a pilgrimage right across south Wales from Tintern Abbey, through lands that were once traversed by the Celtic saints.

The Celtic saints were travellers by nature. Roman Christianity arrived in Britain when the Pope sent Augustine here to preach. But Celtic Christianity had arrived before then and by a very different path. Coming from the Eastern Mediterranean along the trade routes, reaching first into Ireland, then spreading along the sea coasts of the Celtic lands, it was brought by monks who created a network of tiny sites of prayer and preaching wherever they landed. By the twelfth century, one of those sites, St Davids, would be made an official site of Christian pilgrimage by Pope Calixtus the Second: two journeys to St Davids, he said, could be regarded as worth one journey to Rome. But long before that papal pronouncement, in the time of Dewi Sant himself, South Wales had been criss-crossed by the paths of the Celtic saints and their disciples.

Robin Reeves first became an acquaintance of mine, a kind of literary friend, through the back-and-forth process that transpires when magazine articles are submitted and either rejected or accepted, and suggestions for future themes are discussed. The comments and responses of a sympathetic and thoughtful editor, such as Robin showed himself to be as editor of the *New Welsh Review*, provide abiding food for thought and reflection. It was an additional great pleasure to discover Robin's own deep interest in the area and in themes which had long provided me with material for research and thought and writing. His interest took a more practical form than mine – I have never been a walker, except in the mental realm. It is wonderful to know that, following the sad fact of his too early death, Robin's idea for a pilgrimage walk across south Wales to St Davids has received so much support. In the future, many more people may well experience the effort and the awe and the beauty of pilgrimage.

David W. James, St Davids, 2002

Pilgrim Way

remembering Robin Reeves
editor and mountaineer

A hesitant face, a man from the winds
Whose speciality was rock, and paths through rock,
Yet shaped like a stream bed in the trembling sands,
Weather, and gravity, lightning, dark . . .

A journalist must ride Time like a bronco
And the times were not good. Wales in '79
A depleted world, frightened of itself. Echoes
Of Cilmeri rubbished our leaf like acid rain.

Yet he had time, and the integrity of a pilgrim,
To saddle himself to the journey. The dirt road
To nationality out of tribal mayhem
Continually reaches dead end. As poetries fade,

He, whose speciality was rock, paths through rock,
Citizen of Tyddewi, unblocked the track.

Tony Conran

AGAINST THE GALE

Jim Perrin

AGAINST THE GALE

'. . . to hold that one particular conception of the world and of life has in itself a superior capacity for foresight is a mistake of the crudest fatuity and superficiality.'

Antonio Gramsci

'In Tintern in the year 1568 brass was first made by alloying copper with zinc.' I read that on the menu of the Abbey Tearooms whilst making slight inroads into a dull and stodgy toasted teacake awash with melted butter and the size of a *nouvelle cuisine* dinner-plate. Tintern's a brassy place still. Outside, beyond the steamed-up tea-room window, fragile and tottering women with sparse and tinted hair clashed and meshed adjustable walking sticks and clutched bags of mementoes as they struggled down slippery wooden steps to waiting charabancs; dapper jackdaws pecked jauntily across the lawn; the eyes of sated Americans, wearily intent on cramming another old site into their new-world-consciousness, glazed behind glinting round spectacles; beponded goldfish waddled through viscous water; the river frothed reddish-brown and surging around the piers of a rusting box-girder bridge; and rain poured down on tourist, jackdaw, goldfish and hopeful emergent walker alike.

Why so worried, sisters, why?
Sing the silver bells of Wye.

The visitant crowds were heading for the abbey. I joined them, dawdling past the Abbey Mill Shop, that sells carved elephants and cut-glass; past the Abbey Studio, that had a hastily-executed oil painting for sale of a strawberry on a fork; past a yellow plastic notice that invited me to stay another day and enjoy a village lunch ('proceeds in aid of the hall'); down the road to the ruin. Was it for this that not one but many of the great artistic names of the Romantic Period – Gray, Turner, Wordsworth, Palmer – came adventuring to this once-remote place?

Probably not. If the officials in charge of restoration have their way, Tintern Abbey will soon look as new-minted as it must have done after its foundation by the Marcher Lord Fitz Richard from Chepstow in 1131. I have a huge Victorian framed photograph of the abbey, all hanging ivy and dusky light, the quality of its carved capitals and columns and tracery enhanced somehow by their semi-concealment. Today the limestone glowered sullen and damp from underneath scaffolding and green plastic sheeting, hidden again. You could almost imagine that something was finally being done about the complaint made by the Reverend William Gilpin in 1770, that the 'gabel-ends . . . hurt the eye with their regularity and disgust it by the vulgarity of their shape. A mallet judiciously used (but who durst use it?) might be of service in fracturing some of them.' The forthright old apostle of the picturesque has a point, I suppose. All Cistercian rigour and purpose and spiritual aspiration having passed long centuries ago, why should not we, who come merely to stand and gawp and be fed (or have administered by audio-tour) an indigestible mix of fact and interpretation and 'historical re-creation', have the right to tailor the ruin to the purposes of our own imaginations, rather than to those of 'education' and 'marketing' (and profit, ultimately, of course), as CADW, the body that stewards the place, is doing? No longer, as Samuel Palmer had found it, 'trellised with ivy and rising from a wilderness of orchards,' its restoration seems somehow to rob it of its significance and encase the spiritual in the concrete. Patrick Leigh Fermor understands the point:

> . . . for us in the West, because of all such relics they are the most compelling mementoes of the life that once animated them, the ruined abbeys . . . that have remained desolate since the Reformation will always be the most moving and tragic. For there is no riddle here. We know the function and purpose of every fragment and the exact details of the holy life that should be sheltering there. We know, too, the miserable and wanton story of their destruction and their dereliction, and have only to close our eyes for a second for the imagination to rebuild the towers and pinnacles and summon to our ears the quiet rumour of monkish activity and the sound of bells

melted long ago. They emerge in the fields like the peaks of a
vanished Atlantis drowned four centuries deep. The gutted cloisters
stand uselessly among the furrows and only broken pillars mark the
former symmetry of aisles and ambulatories. Surrounded by elder-
flower, with their bases entangled in bracken and blackberry and
bridged at their summits with arches and broken spandrels that fly
spinning over the tree tops in slender trajectories, the clustering
pillars suspend the great empty circumference of a rose-window in
the rook-haunted sky. It is as though some tremendous Gregorian
chant had been interrupted hundreds of years ago to hang there
petrified at its climax ever since.'[1]

It seems that officialdom in our literal age can no longer allow us to
make those bargains between imagination and entropy. I left the all-
encompassing plastic sheeting of this dismal, tourist-trap departure-
point for a pilgrimage behind me, and turned to the gradual ascent out
of the valley of the Wye that leads alongside the Angidy River.
Rhododendron and honesty marked the confines of the village, a lane
led me away, campion, buttercup and cow-parsley masking out the last
pungent flower-heads of ramson along its verges. A 'restored' ironworks
below the road was once again becoming weed-grown, its shorn-up
remnants unvisited and forlorn. Hunched into my waterproofs I
splashed along past Tintern Cross – nothing monumental or symbolic
here, just a meeting of roads – and paced my stride to the beat of
Wordsworth's blank verse:

> Once again I see
> These hedge-rows, hardly hedgerows, little lines
> Of sportive wood run wild; these pastoral farms
> Green to the very door; and wreaths of smoke
> Sent up, in silence, from among the trees,
> With some uncertain notice, as might seem,
> Of vagrant dwellers in the houseless woods,
> Or of some hermit's cave, where by his fire
> The hermit sits alone.

We all refer to the poem as 'Tintern Abbey', and miss out the qualifying 'lines written . . . a few miles above'. Maybe Wordsworth didn't like the place either. Certainly my mood was improving, despite the continuing downpour, with every step I took away from it. The green at the very door of the 'pastoral farms' was *Metallic Amazon* or *Opalescent Viridian* paint on the Saabs and Mercedes parked outside them. Most had brass carriage-lamps by the porch. A few had old lamp-posts and painted wagon wheels. At Trelleck Cross, peaceful and broken among honeysuckle, horse-chestnut and bluebells, the stepped plinth bore a brief octagonal shaft of rough red sandstone. The village of Trelleck a mile beyond – once the county town of Monmouthshire – is a clematis-and-aubrieta-and-neighbourhood-watch kind of place, its cottages and medical centre prim and assured, its church large and fine-facet-steepled, an outer ring of grand old granges surrounded now by the ugly ancillary structures of industrial farming that abut the motte of a vanished marcher castle. 'Tump Terret' it's called, and by tradition was believed to be the burial place of followers of Harold Godwinson who were killed in one of the innumerable border skirmishes that marked the last years of Edward the Confessor's reign. Their Saxon souls would rest easy here, for this is a most English village. The supposed grave mound looks down on three tall red sandstone monoliths, 'Harold Stones', on the other side of the road, mysterious and prehistoric in this household landscape, the usual diabolic folklore attaching to them.

I wanted to avoid Monmouth and all its enforced history lessons, so turned west from Trelleck into the spearing rain and hurried down car-free lanes with illuminated banks of stitchwort and bluebell. At Croes Robert no cross was visible, but any amount of free range eggs, poultry and waterfowl were offered for sale, and the ground fell away to Cwmcarfan, where another cross in the churchyard, grandiosely restored as a war memorial in 1921, rose from a shaft-base identical to the one at Trelleck. Three labourers' cottages beyond the churchyard had been knocked into one, voile curtains draped across the windows, and a sign on a barn door offered free admission for Cwmcarfan residents and friends to the Jubilee BBQ, 'Burgers/Bangers/Chicken drumsticks/Veg. alternative/Bar and Raffle/Red, White and Blue outfits welcome'. The hills of this lush country of the lower Wye were behind me now as I jogged down to the valley of the Trothy, crossed the Fishguard trunk road by a narrow bridge, and just beyond the prosperous old farmhouse of Hendre, took to the fields and the Offa's Dyke Path.

A footbridge crossed a brook to a meadow in the fork between it and the main stream. A herd of cattle with huge, spreading horns, pale fawn hides with silver spots, black noses and ears, and red tags on the latter that enhanced an already magical appearance crowded round me, snuffling and shying briefly away as I reached out to caress them. I walked down to the confluence, attended by them, and looked around. The fairy cattle seemed to follow my gaze. There was nothing for either of us to see but Canada Geese and Mallard ducks feeding across the sodden grass. Yet when Thomas Cromwell's commissioners presented their report in 1536, prior to the dissolution of the monasteries, they wrote of the Cistercian House of Grace Dieu in this field, that 'the Churche, the Quyer, the Cloysters be fayer and the rest of the house in very good repayer and well mayntayned and kept up but of no stately buyldyng.'

They further noted that the priory of Austin canonesses here 'hold in reverence the girdle and part of the tunic of St. Francis, which are supposed to help lying-in women', that two of them had been incontinent and borne children, and that there were fifteen with the prioress, 'of good and virtuous conversation and living; all desire to continue their religion there and none to have capacities.' So their tiny community was reprieved, unlike those of many larger monasteries. Today, every physical trace of its existence is entirely gone. What happened to the sisters subsequently is unknown to history. Most probably, with no new members joining the order, the little abbey no longer an object of pilgrimage, its funds unreplenished after the Acts of Ten Articles and Six Articles, the community aged and died, its relics were taken, its stones removed, the bones of its nuns laid to rest under the sweet grass. The site on which it stood, its tranquillity, its remove, the beauty of its name, the quiet rippling of the iris-bordered stream, the bosomy enclosing hills, all speak more clearly of the 'sense sublime/ Of something far more deeply interfused' that is at the heart of religion than Tintern's grander ruins ever can. A modest holiness lingers here. I said goodbye to the companionable cattle, the geese and ducks, wished a blessing of St. Francis upon their existence in this benign place, crossed the Abbey Bridge, and trudged on through the rain to the wayside medieval church of Llanfihangel Ystern Llewern – St. Michael's of the Fiery Meteor – where I sheltered in the porch awhile, read the notice advising of the forthcoming meeting of Llantilio Crossenny Community Council (9: Highway/footpath matters . . . 13: Burial Board matters . . .) and pondered the way ahead.

What, I wondered, does it mean to be a pilgrim, and why had I undertaken this journey, that so reeks of the self-proclamations of 'spiritual improvement', of the habits of those who crack their knees for no more serious purpose than to be thought better than the rest of us – the spiritual materialists, the self-styled gurus? At an obvious level, my purpose was to record a debt of gratitude and to remember Robin Reeves, whose idea this book had been – to accord him the affection and respect owing to him as mentor and friend. But that motive opens a door on infinite complexity. Bunyan's verses chorus through: 'Hobgoblin nor foul fiend/Can daunt his spirit,/He knows he at the end/Shall life inherit./Then fancies fly away,/He'll fear not what men say,/He'll labour night and day/To be a pilgrim.' I think of the lives like Robin's that have gone before, and their exemplary aspects that deserve our reverence. I think of the heyday of pilgrimage in the centuries between the fall of Rome and the Reformation, the sense of a restless movement of the people searching for Grace. I think of us in our generations, seeking, seeking: '. . . in great resorts;/In cities, theatres, gardens, parks and courts:/At length I heard a ragged noise and mirth . . .' I think of the simple objects of veneration, like the supposed fragments of St. Francis's tunic at Grace Dieu bringing comfort to women in their fear before giving birth, and my mind drifts to the relieved astonishment I felt at my own daughter's safe delivery. Into the porch curls the faint, sweet triethylamine fragrance of the surrounding may blossom. Reminded, I dream of a warm day in the green months, lying at lunchtime on a blanket on the lawn; and later, in the cool of evening, my daughter's mother telling me of how she sat at work that afternoon, listening to patients, her attention undercut by the musk of

our lovemaking, the ripples of remembered pleasure spreading spasmal through her flesh. A stilling of the breeze thickens the may scent to unbearable sweetness, takes me back to my young self at my father's bedside in the Salford hospital where he died; his handsome face wasted on the pillow, not yet fifty but all geniality and life drained from it; the hasty doctors, reductive and philistine, abusing their vested power to condescend and dissemble to the watching child; spreading cancers cutting off the flow of blood to blackening legs that rotted and stank. I set my own in motion, gratefully, and head for Pandy along lanes of northern Gwent flounced with white billows of Queen Anne's Lace and sequined with rain:

> Brave flowers, that I could gallant it like you
> And be as little vaine,
> You come abroade, and make a harmlesse shew,
> And to your beds of Earthe againe.

The way takes me past White Castle, that some have called beautiful. Like a man or woman who smiles on the world and behind closed doors batters the one they profess to love, its charm is a lie. This is a monument to brute force, fear, exclusion, avarice, and none of us should rejoice in those things. Signs advise you of 'Vale of Usk Car Park Watch', warn you that the gates will be locked at 5 p.m. and enjoin you not to use barbeques in the castle and to join Heritage Wales today. I mutter brusque rejoinders and pass swiftly through, hurrying on to Caggle Street, and beyond that Llangattock Lingoed, where the Hunter's Moon Inn briefly tempts, but with two miles only to my destination for the day I resist, climb steps into fields, slant down into an exquisite hidden valley frilled with may, and toil by muddy paths into Pandy. In the Pandy Inn four young women lean over the bar and discuss food and wine, engagement and marriage:

'If you were going out with a married man . . .'

I sit in a corner with my pint of beer, damply, and think of the man for whom I have made this diversion. Raymond Williams, who died in 1988, was born here to a railway signalman and his wife in 1921. That fact's worth any number of miles on foot to me. He's one of those writers whose examples are most searchingly educative: the socially engaged academic and critic whose sense of meaning and resonance is acutely attuned; the essayist whose dialectical toughness expresses and refines an amelioristic world-view; a novelist of great tact, sensitivity, and imaginative and descriptive power; and a teacher – a provider of a model for living – of crucial significance. From when, as an undergraduate thirty years ago, I first came across the cool, principled lucidity of *Culture and Society 1780-1950,* with its fervent extensions and qualifications of the Arnoldian strictures against materialism, I warmed to that distinctive, reasoned voice arguing on the side of the angels and against all the social devils that so insidiously assail us. He's the kind of writer – like William Hazlitt – to whom, for their human qualities, you come to turn and return with expectant delight as an inspiring friend. I'd come to Pandy because – barely disguised – this is the setting for the first novel in his trilogy, *Border Country,* which seems to me an extraordinary, an exemplary piece of writing, the power and the wisdom of it growing on me as I age myself. It's essentially a novel of childhood eliding into one of education, a *bildungsroman* merging into an *erziehungsroman.* But the focus is both sharp and wide, the relationship between father, son and society, the influences upon them, considered with calm gravity and bodied forth with precise delicacy and good sense. The mirroring of lives, the perpetuation of moral qualities in different contexts – these are necessarily of primal concern to anyone who has children, and I know of no better exploration of the themes than in this quiet, contemplative masterpiece.

Yet even this sound critic and wise, perceptive man, mellowing into syncretism, in accommodating himself to the intellectual temper of that vile decade, the 1980s, seemed to lose his bearings. My friend the Gower poet Nigel Jenkins, 'sleek as a seal/With a voice like the waves of the sea' – the man with the most beautiful speaking voice in Wales – worries succinctly at the same point: 'He bizarrely caught the same "postmodern" disease as the problematisers of bullshit, and seemed thereafter to offer little more than scientizing impenetrabilities. Why he should have fallen for this critical fad puzzles me greatly.'

In the Pandy Inn meanwhile, five plump and chip-devouring youths were discussing the mechanical detail of 220 b.h.p. Audi TTs and the suspension of MGF roadsters whilst casting an occasional wistful glance at the girls' bottoms lined up along the bar. Life carries on in its usual ways, catches us on the dilemma of inclusivity. I thought better of asking if anyone here had known Raymond Williams or his father: 'Although he got on easily with his mates at work, he still had no close friends in the village. He never went to the pubs, and his gardens, added to the railway work, left him little free time.'[2] Cultivation and culture – the two seemed suddenly not so far apart, and far closer than many most recent usages and definitions of the latter.

★   ★   ★

Morning, and at last, briefly, the sun shines. To the south rises Ysgyryd Fawr, 'the Holy Mountain, the blue peak with the rockfall on its western scarp'.[3] Wreathed in mist the previous evening, it had looked phantasmal, eerie, impossibly steep, the great landslip cleft on its weather-slope gothically accentuated and strange. In daylight, despite its summit's lowly altitude of 1596 feet, it still has a striking and noble presence. I approach it by way of the grassy shoulder of Arwallt, zig-zag up a steep bracken flank, and arrive on a twisting ridge leading to the top. Two squat pillars of sandstone give entry to the site of St. Michael's Chapel here, the Ordnance Survey pillar standing within confines of which only clear suggestion of a ground plan remains. As late as 1676 the Pope of the day, Clement X, decreed that plenary indulgences would be granted to pilgrims visiting the chapel at Michaelmas. I can remember a large wooden cross thirty years ago, but it has gone, along with much of the mountain-top earth. Several of the churches of Gwent were said to be built on mounds of this, taken particularly from within the chapel, where the soil was so holy that it was scattered on farms round about for good luck and on coffins at Catholic burials. Worm or slug could not live in it, according to some writers – and certainly the only worm I saw on the summit looked in poor shape, so I dug it into deep, moist soil lower down the hill. The superstitions all derived from the massive landslip to the west, that by tradition had occurred when the veil of the temple was rent at Christ's crucifixion. Who knows when it happened in fact? There are other huge landslips in the local sandstone – particularly by Cwmyoy in the Vale of Ewyas. What you can say with certainty is that the view from Ysgyryd Fawr must have thrilled and absorbed any pilgrim. Hills crowd in on every side. To the west, beyond the bracken whale's-back of Deri and the humped dome of the Sugar Loaf, is a harsher, half-hidden land. Eastward lies a rich patchwork of hedged and copsed and tilled red fields with tidy farms and scattered cottages. South is the closing channel of Severn Sea, Somerset beyond it, and to the north and north-east hill upon hill: Herefordshire Beacon, Brown Clee, the Shropshire Hills, the Black Mountains, the distant Berwyn. They pressed in on me the consciousness that I was leaving the soft borderlands behind, moving into different terrain. 'On a May mornynge   on Maluerne hulles/Me byfel a ferly of feyry me thoughte.'4 I plunged on down, through the suburban estates of Abergavenny, over the Sugar Loaf and into Crickhowell, eager to find what lay ahead.

In Crickhowell I had a visit to make. From some forgotten source I'd gleaned the information that Sir George Everest, the former Surveyor-General of India who was certainly born nearby, was also buried in the churchyard here. His name had imperially usurped a perfectly good Tibetan one for the World's highest mountain, and in our own time stood for a strange confusion between capitalism, geography and 'conquest' on the part of investment bankers, consultant surgeons and their ilk for being guided, in return for tens of thousands of dollars or pounds, to the summit of Chomolungma, and – the elements in that part of the world being unruly and capricious – not infrequently dying on the way up or the way down. Penis enlargement would come cheaper, but what the women would do who also indulge in the craze is anybody's guess. That texture aside, these old India hands sometimes have fascinating epitaphs, so I spent a fruitless half-hour clearing away weeds and reading inscriptions before repairing inside the church to avoid a shower. A notice in the porch asked the homeless to come in and take blankets left there for them in the children's corner. Middle-aged men clacked through on shod heels to pray and light candles in the transept chapel. Two painted panels of cherubs, trumps and lyres, collies lying down with lambs and flooding golden light bore an inscription suggesting that, along with the artist's enjoyment of Crickhowell, their inspiration was this passage from *The Song of Songs*:

> My beloved spake, and said unto me, Rise up, my love, my fair one, and come away. For, lo, the winter is past, and the rain is over and gone . . .

I went to the door to check up on the assertion. It was true. The clouds had cleared. I went outside, and on the notice by the gate saw three telephone numbers for clergy. Why not ask about the Everest grave, I thought, and took out my mobile phone. No answer from the first. At the second number, a light-voiced young woman replied in the strangulated vowels of southern England. Awfully sorry. Never heard of him. How very interesting. Simply have no idea. I thanked her politely, rang off, and walked on out of town across the thirteen-arched bridge over the rain-swollen River Usk.

The Monmouthshire and Brecon Canal scores across the hillside to the south. I climbed up to it and set off along the towpath, in which gaping holes were appearing. Bluebells spread across the floor of a beechwood on the farther bank, shafts of sunlight transmuting their colour to shimmering flame. From the topmost branch of a holly tree a mistle thrush sang into the rising storm that was scattering blossom across the slow, brown water. Round the first bend an orange pippin of a man, cheeks blotched carmine and sere, came bustling towards me armed with large golfing umbrella and a video camera:

'You seen the 'oles, then? You seen the 'oles . . ?'

Round the next bend, I told him, four hundred yards at most.

'Something to tell 'em when I get 'ome,' he rattled, brandishing the video camera, and stumbled on excitedly.

The little, unpretentious flowers of spring thronged the shady grasses, and the air was full of nymphs flying with body vertical and a whirr of wings. I came across Essex Man sucking at a lager can in the stern of his narrow boat, that was pulled up against the bank. A fishing line dangled over the side. He was glowering ahead at a fallen ash tree across the canal: '. . . fackinblockmiteoirennemonamowboyl – aycamminacleeri' . . .' I left him waiting there, unhappy and impatient, gulping at the tin teat, float of his line drifting away soft and slow. Four ducklings jerked and dabbed among twigs and leaves of the ash tree, parents nowhere in sight. Two buzzards wheeled and mewed overhead. In a field this side of the river I focus on a brown shape at the edge of the bracken by a boundary stream:

> The hare, crouched in her form,
> Listens to the whispering world.
> Its dry, husked grasses speak
> Of approaching stealth;
> Leaf-fall's a foot's soft tread,
> Stream over stones
> Is the murmur of men.
>
> All's danger here. She bounds away,
> Halts on the low ridge,
> Ears swivel back, she turns –
> Her misted eye clouds
> Over sunlit empty land;
> Heel-mark by a thorn hedge
> Holds the sleeping leveret.

Even our new-born are threatened by fears we imagine or amplify, by the scarred retinas of experience; so damage self-perpetuates. I see two rabbits, lined up, and think of the time when with one shot I might have taken them for the pot. Into my mind comes Flaubert's intense, redemptive re-working of The Golden Legend. The rabbits hop forward into sunlight and I pass on. Across the valley the Italianate tower, red-brick-topped, of some absurdly grandiloquent house stands out. Shades of Tuscany. The river curves away from it, to run beneath where I walk. In Llangynidr the school pick-up run has begun, Shoguns and Fronteras and Discoverys driven by groomed women with blonde highlights are packing into the cul-de-sacs. I head for the Red Lion. 'Are you open?' I ask the landlady.

'Well . . .' She looks me up and down, '. . . for another five minutes, maybe. What would you like . . ?'

'You,' I feel like saying. She's tousled and funny and full of life. I glance along the bar. 'Pint of the Reverend James, please,' is what passes my lips, 'and do you have any sandwiches?'

'I'll make you one,' she smiles, and repeats again that tantalising formula.

'Whatever's easiest.'

Two minutes later she's back with a stacked plate of good, clean food.

'Sit down here. It's alright. I won't shut. It's just that I got soaked in Abergavenny this morning, see, and I'll have to go upstairs and tidy myself up . . .' She flicks the cascading curls. '. . . and I need to take a shower before we open up for the evening. Would you like pickle?'

I shake my head, thank her, take my pint and food outside into the fading sun and the strengthening wind. Kind women are a gift in this life, to be treated kindly. She locks the door behind me. I sit at a table in the sheltered garden, the scent of honeysuckle all around me, and am ridiculously happy. A terracotta green man smiles down from under a laburnum tree on the pansies and the pinks, and a harassed-looking blonde woman walks across the lawn.

'Is the landlady in?'

'I think she'll be down in a few minutes.'

'Oh, I'll wait then. I'm new, see – first week covering this area – Castell Howell Foods, Carmarthen,' she explains.

She's still waiting as I leave. By Sardis United Reformed Church ('formerly the Congregational Chapel') – services at 9.30 every Sunday with the Reverend Shem Morgan – I branch hillwards, but not before looking into the neat and flowery graveyard behind, with its view towards the Black Mountains from under the spreading yew, the UPVC windows looking down on it, the rows of Bevans and Watkins and Merediths, and the pinky-purple delaminating Silurian rocks of its wall. The lane I follow is bordered with wallflower and forget-me-not. '*Acaena Mycrophilia*' reads the tag on one raised bed. The cottages are neat, empty, prosperous, expensively furnished, sun-terraced, devoid of books, and the coming gale is thrashing in the lilac and laburnum trees around them. I climb the lane, leaving this dormer village of rich rural dreams behind me, the back of my hand absent-mindedly brushing against nettles as I go. Looking at the red weals raised, I concentrate on the stinging, find a curious, expectation-confounding affirmation rather than unpleasantness in the tingling sensation. A wasp lands among the weals and totters back and forth, inspecting me with its antennae. I study its gorgeous patterning before it flies erratically away. An uphill mile brings me to a path that forks south-west to follow the stream's course. From the last building standing at the old *tyddyn* of Blaen y Cwm, an elder grows from a windward wall and a corner has fallen away. All's abandoned here, and the sheep surviving from last year's carnage bawl round it raucously, no good shepherd to tend to them now, some already shedding across the rough pasture fleeces that once were a valued commodity. Heart-leaves of the celandine, so late in flower at this height, carpet the mirey sunken way ahead, boulders of its walls downy with moss. Tiring now, with the storm gathering around me and the traverse of the moor ahead, I catch at my own studied movement as I cross steps of a stile slick with algae, think that I have seen the old dance thus, carefully – but still, they dance. Behind me, a rainbow spans Llangynidr, rain drenches down on a whirling wind, and ring-ousels pipe and dip along the last pools of the stream before I broach the moor.

> *To the south things are sullen,*
> *Say the pink bells of Brecon.*

This moor – Llangynidr Mountain it's called – I have been here before, climbed on its rimming rocks in soft summer days, crawled far below the surface in labyrinthine underground passages, walked its heather, visited the Chartist Cave out of respect for those who sheltered there, after the Merthyr Rising of 1831 at the time of the martyrdom of Dic Penderyn who died with the single word, 'Injustice!', on his lips, and at other times of foment and oppression in the industrial history of The Valleys. Today the cloud is down, and I look across the moor's high expanse with some anxiety. There are paths – two or three of them – marked on the map, but I know each of them to be discontinuous, conjectural, no more than expressions of legal license and cartographic hope. I have no compass to make this crossing. Out of the shelter of the valley the wind is blasting and wuthering and the ground is rough – knee-deep heather and bilberry over most of it, shake-holes where the underground caverns have collapsed, swallow-holes where the brief streams disappear, scatters of boulders, fields of slippery rocks. There is a sense about it that few now come this way, few make the crossing in either direction. By instinct, helped by occasional glimpses through scudding cloud of a veiled sun, I head south. The lash of rain pricks at my eyeballs. I feel the blast of wind – so strong at times as to bowl me into the heather – as almost a soft touch; but overlaid with cold points of pain. Sheep-paths through leads in the heather interlink, veer away in roughly the right quarter. The wind ever more violent, I have to blink into it to spy out the way, then thrust onwards. I think of the chambers and stream-passages underground into which the surface water, through cracks and crannies dissolved out of the rock, trickles and pours, its fierce, flooding rush down there like the power of our emotions, all swirl and confusion, devoid of light. Two figures resolve out of the mist in front of me, one tall, with a massive head and the bulky shoulders and barrel chest of a miner, gesticulating, stopping momentarily to hammer points home with rock-like fists; the other darting, puckish, a will-o'-the-wisp. I hasten to catch them and as I draw close the big man fades into shreds of cloud as though he had never been, and the voice of the little one is murmuring behind the wind, 'He liked to run away from Bedlam. He liked to have all the harness taken off him.' A gap opens in the mist. Down there I see the straggling terraces of Beaufort, and catch a glimpse of the two of them again, toiling up here against the gale of the world, icy blasts of contempt at their back. '1929,' the wind hisses, 'that old unseated officialdom, the incumbents whose fire burns only in their self-importance, the ones with power to lose – no breath of mine was ever as cold as theirs':

[After the miners' nomination] his first meeting was in Beaufort. It started in dead silence and ended in dead silence. He stammered badly, and, according to Archie Lush, made the worst speech of his life. That night the two friends went on one of their favourite walks across the Llangynidr Mountain, with Aneurin wondering whether it was wise to persist . . .[5]

Michael Foot, in the two volumes of *Aneurin Bevan 1897-1960* that together constitute the most affectionate, lucid and generous-hearted political biography of the twentieth century, tells of 'the walks across the mountains, ten, fifteen or twenty miles in a day' of Bevan's youth. As I drop down towards the industrial estates along the Heads of the Valleys Road, I think of the potent cultural mix of that time: David Bevan's copy of *The Clarion* in the house every week, with its stress on egalitarianism, intellectual self-improvement and the open air; the library encounters with Thoreau's and Shelley's idealism; the novels of Conrad; the Hegelian philosophy of F.H. Bradley (whose father's sermons had rung out from under the silver bells of Glasbury-on-Wye beyond the moor and the Black Mountains to the north); the musical and singing tradition of The Valleys. With all that colour and texture of thought and rhetoric dancing in my head, I plashed and skidded down the last mile of waterlogged ground to gain the old tramway running round from Trefil, a landscape opening up to the south bleakly and utterly different from those I had crossed on the other side of this harsh barrier.

The mines and quarries they once served long defunct, the engines that hauled along them gone for scrap, these level, high belvederes contouring the hill-scarps are green tracks now. With relief, I turned east and surfed with the gale at my back down to Nant y Croft. Seven burnt-out cars rusted in a gully beneath the tramway. Cases of used shotgun cartridges were littered around. A battered white Transit van parked outside the first houses carried the bird-brained-dog symbol of the British Association for Shooting and Conservation. I ignored a pub, crossed the bridge over the Heads of the Valleys Road, found marked public paths blocked off where the land they crossed had been acquired for more of the box-like, vast, subsidised factories, pylons that crackled in the mist crossing the grass and scrub towards them. The rain and wind slashed ever more savagely across a soured upland of waste and slag and industrial lagoons, lapwings careened and screamed on the turbulent air, a buffeted heron flapped slowly away from the tormented, gunmetal surface of one of the ponds:

Now it is May in all the valleys,
Days of the cuckoo and the hawthorn,
Days for splashing in the mountain ponds . . .

Idris Davies's lyrical description was unrecognisable on a day like this. Soaked to the skin, teeth chattering with cold, stopped in my tracks at times by the wind, I battled along the road and came to the exposed high promontory at Waun y Pound where the Aneurin Bevan memorial is to be found.

Under a wooden shelter is a picture of the great orator, speaking to a crowd of men and women, their attention rapt, their faces excited, their dress meagre and poor. Beyond are the stones, big, rough-hewn, weathered limestone blocks, square and solid, four in number. There is one each for the major communities of his parliamentary constituency: Ebbw Vale, Tredegar, Rhymney. The central and largest one is for Nye himself, and bears this simple inscription:

From this point Aneurin Bevan spoke to the people of his constituency and the world.

It's pocked by air-gun pellets, some letters illegible, and take-away cartons and Special Brew cans are strewn across the track from the car-park. There's a harsher tone to the voice in the wind now, and its disaffected burden runs thus: 'What the fuck are politicians to us? Any politicians? Even this politician..? Look what they done to us, mun, and look what they left us with . . .' I look around me, at these austere sheds of factories planted on the desolate moors and with all the signs around them of under-production and short-time; at the homes that were close to the industry, so there the people must live, clinging to the sides of valleys funnelling up every gale that blew from Severn Sea; and I think of the battles Nye Bevan fought: against militarism and the setting of working men of nations into conflict with each other; with the mine-owners who had, despite the Sankey recommendations, resumed so malevolently parsimonious a control over the mines after the Great War; with that 'new race of robbers', the Poor Relief Commissioners, after the General Strike of 1926; with those who espoused non-intervention in the Spanish Civil War; with the Labour Party itself over its policies in the Second World War and on other occasions; with the despotic incompetence that lumbered behind the inflated and bellicose rhetoric of Winston Churchill, and with the rest of a Tory Party he regarded as 'lower than vermin' (God knows – pretty well by now, no doubt – what he would have thought of the cohorts of Thatcherism); with the avarice and autocracy of the medical profession, particularly over nationalisation of the hospitals and the sale of general practices (something that effectively crept in through the back door again during the 'reforms' of the 1980s), in the formulation, before its inception in 1948, of his greatest memorial, the National Health Service – modelled, he would always claim, on the Tredegar Medical Aid Society; for better workers' housing in the great programme of public building during the term of the Attlee Government; with the British press, that he regarded as 'most prostituted in the world'; with the Attlee Government itself over armaments expenditure in a time of social need. That any of these should have been battles . . !

Racked by fits of shivering, rain dripping from me, I turn again into the wind and head down a dismal twilight road, past a squalid pub with its gable end clad in corrugated iron, into Tredegar. And as I go, on to the wind I chant out the peroration from Bevan's last great speech, 'Why I am a Socialist', to the Blackpool Conference after the electoral defeat – any Conservative victory is a people's defeat – of 1959; with a sense of wonder as I do so at its prescience and continuing relevance, and a sad suspicion that no-one with this command of language and firmly principled selfless conviction is active in politics today:

I have enough faith in my fellow creatures in Great Britain to believe that when they have got over the delirium of the television, when they realise that their new homes that they have been put into are mortgaged to the hilt, when they realize that the moneylender has been elevated to the highest position in the land, when they realize that the refinements for which they should look are not there, that it is a vulgar society of which no decent person could be proud, when they realize all those things, when the years go by and they see the challenge of modern society not being met by the

Tories who can consolidate their political powers only on the basis of national mediocrity, who are unable to exploit the resources of their scientists because they are prevented by the greed of their capitalism from doing so, when they realize that the flower of our youth goes abroad today because they are not being given the opportunities of using their skill and their knowledge properly at home, when they realize that all the tides of history are flowing in our direction, that we are not beaten, that we represent the future: then, when we say it and mean it, then we shall lead our people to where they deserve to be led!

Even as the passion of the speech flowed from him, the cancer was within. Eight months of serious illness after delivering it, he – the great visionary politician of my lifetime, 'the most creative and dynamic personality in the Socialist movement of his generation'[6] – was dead. Nye Bevan had 'sailed into his rest;/Savage indignation there/Cannot lacerate his breast./Imitate him if you dare,/World-besotted traveller; he/Served human liberty.' If the Welsh Nation were working towards the just society, instead of no more than an expedient accommodation to the meretricious existing one, study of the life of Aneurin Bevan would be one of the chief objects of its history.

★   ★   ★

It is mid-day, and after my previous day's soaking I'm taking it easy in Tredegar, lounging under the clock tower in The Circle – nothing so bland as a town square for Tredegar. With its square plinth, round column and ornate ironwork it has something of the lighthouse about it, but it just tells the time, gives you the names of Wellington's victories, records the raising of funds for its construction through a bazaar in 1858, has a fine weathercock to show which way the wind blows, and a railed tulip garden beneath in which I'm musing. Opposite me is the town hall of 1818, stone-built and solemn and now the NCB Club. On its steps sit three young teenagers, eating chips in soft white bread rolls from newspaper and talking about what their favourite meal is at MacDonald's. A blue plaque to one side – one of several on the *Aneurin Bevan Heritage Trail* – records that from the balcony above them his first election as member of Parliament was announced on 1 June, 1929. 'The first function of a political leader is advocacy', it continues in Bevan's words. 'It is he who must make articulate the wants, the frustrations and the aspirations of the masses.' The boys chatter on about Big Macs with cheese and fries. The sign down the hill outside Wetherspoon's *The Olympia* – security cameras trained on its entrance – demands proper dress and invites you to 'Steak out all day every day in the Gardd Gwrw'. Clockwise from the plaque, The Circle of Beauty salon advertises 'all aspects of beauty therapy – electrolysis, non-surgical face-lifts, tramsion, nail extensions, wedding packages etc.' The sense of shifting priorities is overpowering. I look back up at the balcony and wonder whether Michael Foot's election victories were announced from here too, whether there's a blue plaque on his constituency home at 10, Nelson Street, Tredegar. I recall the savage vituperation and personal abuse directed by Conservative press and politicians and ignoramuses in saloon bars across the south of England against Foot in his time as leader of the Labour Party, when the values of the mob – incited by a sneering and despicable female mob-orator in the most reductive electoral campaigns in history, unmediated by any notion of altruistic principle, by any standard of moral decency, by any motive other than personal greed and gain – obtained in these islands. I consider my own contacts with the man – his principled generosity, his intellectual excitement, his modesty and humour, the keen and retentive grasp of a cultured mind – contrast these with the preenings and posturings and philistinism of his tormentor-in-chief Margaret Thatcher. And I feel the necessity to record these contexts and observations to set against the slack and amnesiac numerical chronicling of his electoral defeat; and having done so, to leave a changed Tredegar behind:

> *Why must life be so meagre?*
> *Plead the bells of Tredegar.*

Past the old General Hospital where the lungs of generations of miners were coughed out, past a tacky funfair grinding into desultory life, the road curves up past hill-top cemeteries, past the thick-maned shaggy ponies grazing over the Tredegar and Rhymney Golf Club, past the rusty shacks and burnt-out cars on to the moor before descending into Rhymney itself, with its Garden City, its pigeon lofts, its Health and Fitness Centre, its Puddlers' Arms and its Rhymney Silurian Choir.

Oh what can you give me?
Say the sad bells of Rhymney.

What I was given was the steep road out of Pontlottyn on to Cefn y Brithdir, and I had come up here for a particular reason. But first, there is the opportunity to look around, for this ridge is as good a near viewpoint as any into The Valleys. In that broken, falling ground away to the west, the industry that was its ruin itself gone, are Merthyr Tydfil, Dowlais Top, Penywern – the latter birthplace to The Valleys' most passionate modern historian, Gwyn Alf Williams, who taught of human experience and its meaning until the pain of all that witness gave way to whisky's anaesthesia and – far too soon – he died:

It was . . . a place of warmth and fellowship and challenge; a centre of genuine intellectual liveliness, of drama societies, readings, eisteddfodau, above all a place dedicated to intellectual self-improvement as its members conceived it, devoted to the readings of books (in any language)[7]

Below me, running down to the south and east, is the Rhymney Valley, the ridges beyond it enclosing Sirhowy and Ebbw Vale and Blaina. Euro-millions have smoothed over the industrial scarring, in collaboration with nature have brought the land back to some semblance of its pre-industrial green. But the evidence of these communities' dispossession, the erasure of social hope here in the last two decades, is palpable. I look across them and see concrete proof of the eighteen years of annual compound Conservative disinvestment in – what Margaret Thatcher, in her most chilling phrase, told us did not exist – society. I see clear illustration of the statistic that in 1979, nine per cent of Britons lived below the official poverty line, and in the year

2000 the figure had leapt to a quarter of the population, the crossings of the barriers out of that state had been made ever more difficult, whilst at the other end of the spectrum the rich had grown ever richer, and the social differentiations ever more stark. In the bowl of the hill to the north, at an altitude of 1200 feet, the tailings of its former collieries all around them, are the terraces of Fochriw:

> *Fuck you, fuck you, fuck you*
> *Snarl the bells of Fochriw.*

I walk towards them, sense movement among the piles of refuse dumped, scattered and blown across the moor, see a man there, and a dog, both scavenging, an old child's push-chair nearby filled with broken pieces of laminate floorboards. I watch awhile:

> On the ground
> His eyes are turn'd, and, as he moves along,
> They move along the ground; and evermore,
> Instead of common and habitual sight
> Of fields with rural works, of hill and dale,
> And the blue sky, one little span of earth
> Is all his prospect.[8]

I call out a greeting, he looks up, straightens his back and walks over, his dog trotting to heel, snickering its lip a little at the presence of a stranger, rangy and suspicious. The man's stocky, watchful, unshaven, his expression humorous and sidelong. I'd think him about sixty:

'How's it going, mun? I thought you was the DSS for a minute. They'll dock your dole if they find you up here. Wouldn' make that much difference, mind – worth 'alf what it was. Firewood – burns well with the glue in it . . .'

He gestures towards the push-chair, reaches in the pocket of his torn ski-jacket, brings out a pouch of Golden Virginia, rolls a cigarette and offers me the pouch.

'You out walkin'. . ? Not the prettiest place, by 'ere.'

I tell him where I've been, where I'm going. We squat down in the heather out of the wind, smoking and talking. I take chocolate and bananas out of my rucksack, share them with him

'I been out o' work eighteen years, and it's not for want of looking, but at my age they don' want you. I'm lucky, you know, children gone, but it's hard for the younger ones, what with wantin' everythin'. I don't blame them for takin' it sometimes, when they've 'ad so much taken from them. You read in the papers 'ow bad this place is, with the drugs and beatin' our wives and that, and then you see the people on telly all doing the same things, and you read the statistics. You know who's the worst for domestic violence, and that's the worst thing in my book . . ?'

I look at him, shake my head.

'It's not us, up here in Fochriw or over in Merthyr or down in Rhymney. The women are the strength of these places – always 'ave been. It's the doctors and policemen. The women's groups'll tell you that. So what does that say about society, mun? That those on top and in charge are as big a set of fuckin' 'ypocrites as ever they were? Well, I'd better get these off 'ome. Been good talkin' to you, boy.'

He stands up, shakes my hand, collects the push-chair, whistles his dog and sets off along the road, 'endued with sense'. I feel strangely desolate at his going, turn south on the old Roman road that heads for Gelligaer. The wind tumbles a startling blue carton against my foot as I look at the map: 'Aries Ram – super satisfaction guaranteed', it reads, 'soft and flexible, multi-speed. For more information on the use of this product contact www.sexcatalogue.co.uk.'

Gimme that just to slot in,
Shrill the belles of Pontlottyn.

Black plastic like prayer flags streams in the wind from barbed wire above all the moor's discarded objects of brief pride. Around the horizon spread the Sugar Loaf, the Black Mountains, the Brecon Beacons, Mynydd Llangynidr, Fforest Fawr, the Carmarthen Van. Larks are singing above me, and spring is bronzed across the remnant oakwoods above Rhymney. Lambs play among the detritus, ponies glance up in brief wariness, a bedraggled ram nibbles thin and waterlogged grass, nuzzles aside the plastic hand and arm of a child's doll. I find myself suddenly rehearsing the arguments of Marcuse, that I have not read in over thirty years, from his *Essay on Liberation*: on how capital stimulates and debases appetite and aspiration, to serve its own ends and keep the people in thrall. As I do so, an old car pulls up not far ahead. A woman steps from a rear door, smoothing down her skirt as she straightens up. She goes round to the other side, opens it, and helps out a frail, small, stumbling figure, his clothes hanging loosely upon him, a pair of thick-lensed wire-rimmed spectacles, twisting and askew, clinging uncertainly to his nose. He takes her arm and totters up the road. The driver and front-seat passenger remain, talk softly, concernedly. The walking pair have not gone many yards before it becomes too much for the man, and they turn again. Holding on to the woman's arm he slowly makes his way back along the road to the car, and gratefully enters it.

That was the saddest thing I saw during our friendship.[9]

The vision fades, of Idris Davies and Morfydd, his fiancee, just before the poet's death, of cancer at the age of 48 in 1953. He came back here, the miner who'd studied during and after The Strike to become a qualified teacher, only to find the community he'd left irrevocably changed:

It is bitter to know that history
Fails to teach the present to be better than the past.

His poems are why I have come to Rhymney, and why I'm taking this route along the ridgeway of Cefn y Brithdir, where he took his last walk. 'The Valleys' very own folk poet', Professor M. Wynn Thomas — most eclectic and intelligent of modern Welsh literary critics — called him.[10] The fond reference to his rootedness is entirely appropriate, though it's wise to stress too the sophistication and irony evident in Davies's two great poetic sequences, *Gwalia Deserta* and *The Angry Summer*, and to a lesser extent also in the more stylised, fading and elegiac *Tonypandy*. Wynn Thomas's own comment implicitly concedes the point:

. . . the [poetic] sequence has repeatedly demonstrated its ability to accommodate material both socio-political and personal; it has the capacity to bring the one realm of experience into suggestive relationship with the other.

My first encounter with Idris Davies's verse was − ironically − in the Free Trade Hall in Manchester in about 1961, hearing Pete Seeger, the Harvard Communist, sing out his inspiring setting of 'The Bells of Rhymney', that was to remain a folk-revival and folk-rock standard of the 1960s, imprinting the names and the sense of the industrial history of South Wales on the psyche of a generation. A decade on I saw Tony Conran's groundbreaking production of *The Angry Summer* in the little drama studio in Bangor, was overwhelmed by its forceful realisation of what Conran termed 'the greatness of *The Angry Summer* as a dramatic poem'.[11]

Both the major sequences are 'about' the same event − the General Strike of 1926 that was a defining moment in the industrial history of Britain, its continuance in the South Wales Coalfield, and the effect on the society that existed there. The interplay of character, the tonal range, the apparent naivety which conceals a depth of precise knowledge, skill and literary technique in bodying forth the speech and the values and the philosophy of that community, are hallmarks of genius, and indices to works of exceptional moral gravity and force. Even in Wales, the quality of these sequences went long unrecognised. Within the English literary establishment they won a measure of condescension ('. . . the best poetic document I know about a particular epoch in a particular place': T.S.Eliot), and were quickly forgotten:

> The village of Fochriw grunts among the higher hills;
> The dwellings of miners and pigeons and pigs
> Cluster around the little grey war memorial.
> The sun brings glitter to the long street roofs
> And the crawling promontories of slag,
> The sun makes the pitwheels to shine,
> And praise be to the sun, the great unselfish sun,
> The sun that shone on Plato's shoulders,

That dazzles with light the Taj Mahal.
The same sun shone on the first mineowner,
On the vigorous builder of this brown village,
And praise be to the impartial sun.
He had no hand in the bruising of valleys,
He had no line in the vigorous builder's plans,
He had no voice in the fixing of wages,
He was the blameless one.
And he smiles on the village this morning,
He smiles on the far-off grave of the vigorous builder,
On the ivied mansion of the first mineowner,
On the pigeon lofts and the Labour Exchange,
And he smiles as only the innocent can.[12]

With miles still to go, I hurry past the Civil Aviation Authority beacon and down to Capel y Brithdir, high on the hill above New Tredegar. The chapel has long been demolished, its foundations formed into a memorial plinth itself now becoming derelict, the steps askew, ash saplings probing the masonry. I climb the stile into the burial ground and walk among the listing gravestones. The inscriptions for the ridgetop farms are in Welsh, those of the valley in English. One brown marble monument with a cypress growing by it and smaller, fallen, flaking, uninscribed sandstone slabs all around reads thus:

In affectionate remembrance of Margaret Ann, beloved daughter of Joseph and Ann Roberts of New Tredegar, who died December 18th, 1880, aged 18 years, also of Mary, Jane, and John Roberts, who died in infancy. 'We cannot, Lord, thy purpose see,/But all is well that's done by thee.' Also of William Roberts, their son, who died April 10, 1890, aged 32 years. 'In the midst of life, we are in death. A loving son and a true friend.' Also of the above named Ann Roberts, who departed this life February 22nd, 1896 aged 70 years. 'She is not dead but gone before/And beckons us to heaven'. Also of the above-named Joseph Roberts, who died September 14th, 1902, aged 74 years. Thy will be done.

The walled lane beyond twists down into a wood where beech and damson intertwine, the banks of a stream are lined with holly, hazel, birch and rowan and the slope beyond is bright with gorse. Shadow of a buzzard travels the pasture and leads my eye up to huge mounds of spoil above, re-emphasizes the frequent Valleys juxtaposition of the industrial and the old agrarian. I'm put in mind of Vincent Evans' fine allegorical painting of 1935, *A Welsh Family Idyll*,[13] its simple utopianism so clearly evoking a bitter alternative discourse of the artist's and the communities' own experience. Sound of a police siren throbs out of Bargoed. Above outcropping silurian rocks, from a little copse of oak-trees, their leaves a bright yellowy-green darkening now into summer maturity, a green woodpecker suddenly takes flight and dips away with a call like loud and mocking laughter. At Pencaedrain a golf-course is surrounded with razor-wire, and two pastel-fleeced and green-wellingtoned women on the school run lounge against adjacently-parked new sports utility vehicles. In the steel-shuttered and security-grilled VG shop at Gelligaer, where I buy apples and flapjack, the woman who serves me asks where I've come from, where I'm going, gives me directions for the paths, jokes for me to wait here while she runs home to get her boots on. The footpath legacy of the Groundwork Trusts – like the Cotton Famine roads on the Pennine Moors – speaks of manufactured labour at a time of industrial depression or transition. I skirt Nelson, and at seven o'clock arrive in the Greyhound Inn at Llanfabon. The barmaid is extravagantly blonde, exchanges pleasantries with me about the weather, complains about her husband being away golfing in Spain, and serves beer and food to her other customers with phenomenal rapidity and efficiency. Opposite me an elephantine, multiple-jewelled Australian woman discusses house-buying, water-rates, Artex and fitted wardrobes with a woman friend to the accompaniment of disco-beat from a speaker above her head. Location, access, parking? quizzes her friend, as the large woman sips ruminatively at her Bacardi Lime Breezer and stuffs chips from her plate into her mouth by the handful. Above a living-flame gas-fire, diagonal false beams carry a weight of hunting prints and plate-racks and odd bits of tack. A wall clock has stopped at twenty past five. The upholstery is red plush chenille with a print of Latin script. *Ne tentes aut perfice,* it reads – do not strive except for perfection. I finish my pint and set out on the last hour's walk of the day.

It lies across Cefn Eglwysilan. I trail wearily up Ffos yr Haidal, concentrating on the rhythm, putting aside the urge to spin on my heels, admire the view, rest. Around the bronze age cairns of Garneddi Llwydion, where the minor road comes in across Mynydd Eglwysilan, half-a-dozen of the burnt-out cars, uniform rust-coloured, Fiestas and Cavaliers and Astras, are arranged almost artistically across the moor.

Almost artistically . . . In 1999 the Sherman Theatre in Cardiff premiered Blackwood playwright and poet Patrick Jones's first play, *everything must go.* It had music from Cerys Matthews and Catatonia, from the Manic Street Preachers (Patrick's brother Nicky Wire plays in the band), and from Stereophonics. It's devastating, visceral drama:

> See that merc Johnny nicked yesterday, tonned it up Tredegar he did, coppers couldn't catch im he said, good laugh ol Johnny good piss taker – i wouldn't mind getting one myself tonight – saw some smart bmws down chartists view, rich wankers wouldn't miss em if i did anyway – standing there with their posh alarms and crook locks – bollocks – simple as fuck – . . . point is to beat the biz – beat 'em at it like – nick the car – give the coppers a good chase like then ditch it or torch the fucker on the mountain and fuck off back to bed like . . .[14]

A little way on, I climb up from the track and sit on an ancient bank, looking down into the valley to the east. I study the map. Senghenydd Dyke's the bank I'm sitting on. The village down there is Senghenydd itself. Beneath this hill in 1913, after an explosion two thousand feet underground in the Senghenydd Pit, and a fire that raged on for days, four hundred and thirty nine men died. The tragedy concentrated the bitterness of a community against mineowners who continually ignored minimum safety regulations and put profit before any consideration of the welfare of men. Nor did those same mineowners clean up in any other way than that of profits. I wander a few yards west across the moor until I can look down into Cwm Taf. Up the valley, beyond the river's bend at Quaker's Yard, in the encroaching shadows I can just make out the hill cemetery of Aberfan. And I remember as a nineteen-year-old getting a lift into Brecon on that terrible October morning, and hearing on the car radio the first reports of how, at 9.15, after days of rain, the tip above Pant Glas School had begun to slide. A hundred and forty four graves of the victims are in that cemetery, a hundred and sixteen of them children. They were dug out from the sludge and slurry, from classroom and playground, some sitting at desks, some holding hands. Burnt in the depths of the earth. Drowned in black waste. These people and their children. There is a gestural, fearful symmetry in those contemptuous torchings by the ancient cairn.

The track over Cefn Ilan dips south, Severn Sea visible now, and merges into a potholed road veering west. A continual susurrus of police sirens spills out of the valley, cuckoos call across the hillside, the chimes of an ice-cream van ring across some hidden and nearby estate. Close at hand a shotgun's being discharged again and again: *phut, pah! phut, pah! phut, pah!* In front, a sturdy church tower within what looks like a much older churchyard settles like a sleepy cat into its hollow in the hillside, an old pub alongside. The church being locked and the hour growing late, the pub beckons.

Inside the *Rose & Crown* goatee'd, leather-jacketed and shaven-headed men with tight-clad wives drink lager and order 16 oz. rump steaks medium rare with pepper sauce, onion rings, garlic bread and chunky chips: 'I'm going to buy myself a nice Rolex,' one man confides to the other, 'I'll pay eight hundred, a thousand, fifteen hundred quid for it – know a guy who'll fix me up, do me a deal.' The may blossom outside the window is in its glory, catching the last, errant sun. I buy a pint of Buckley's, install myself at a table by the window, go for a piss. In the toilet a young man with extravagant tattoos and startling blue eyes comes in and fastens on me:

'These women, they're fuckin' 'ard work, mun – you know, all I want is to get up on the mountain with a tent an' a few chickens – a few cans, fags, a few spliffs and that's happiness to me – but she want me to work hard, make loads of money – you know, house, kids – I don't want kids, mun – it's not that I can't stand kids, they're great at a distance, but you know – she wants kids, money, all that – what's in it for me but slavery, mun? But if I fuck her off, I look a twat, don't I? If I won the lottery, a few million like, I'd make a twat of myself for a year or two with drugs and prostitutes and that, but then I'd just be up in a house on the mountain with chickens and a few spliffs – that's happiness, mun. Anyway, thanks a lot mate – you're my agony uncle, you are.'

As I go back to my table, an attractive young woman in a low-cut blouse, a pint by the empty chair opposite her, tilts back her head, blows out cigarette smoke, and gives me an expressionless, up-and-down appraisal. A great bear of a German Shepherd Dog lollops over as I sit down, rests a heavy head on my knee and rolls its eyes upwards, begging. Two butchers behind me discuss the formalisation of the sale of meat: 'Every piece of meat that comes into the shop these days, I got to keep a separate log on it, like. Waste o' time . . .' Outside the gale's blowing back in, tearing, blasting. I ponder the writer's role, who has no clear home, and must stand apart, hold up the mirror, observe, work towards a sense of the more harmonious, the more ideal, the better attuned. Inadequately:

> I am a Socialist. That is why I want as much beauty as possible in our everyday lives, and so am an enemy of pseudo-poetry and pseudo-art of all kinds. Too many 'poets of the Left', as they call themselves, are badly in need of instruction as to the difference between poetry and propaganda . . . These people should read Blake on Imagination till they show signs of understanding him. Then the air would be clear again, and the land be, if not full of, fit for song.[15]

★   ★   ★

Today will, I hope, be last of this pilgrimage. The jackdaws are dancing on a wild wind that blows in from Severn Sea, the torn blossom fills the air like snow, the swell of the storm pulses through long meadow grasses. Telephone wires are down, the new leaves whip about, croziers of bracken uncurl from last year's growth. At Nant Garw by the traffic lights a pert, tense-thighed girl on a sturdy chestnut pony jumps red on a busy dual carriageway, makes the central reservation, two lanes of fast traffic on either side. The pony wild-eyed, its nostrils flared, she yanks on the iron bit, turns him in tight circles, exulting in her control. I follow the old railway down towards Cardiff, evidence of things unseen – badger-trails, fox-prints in the mud – all along the abandoned way.

In Tongwynlais an old woman clutches her bag of prescriptions, a young girl presses to her ear a mobile phone. Under the M4 bridge, the gentrified graffiti read, 'Pook Off, Hunt Scum Murderers; Pootle Off, Countryside Alliance; Animal Farmers Are Tossers'. The brown, flooding river rushes down towards the city, infiltrating, cleansing. At Radyr Weir where the water was taken off to Melin Griffith Ironworks, no longer do the rafts of chemical foam rear in the broken waters downstream. Fforest Farm, by the old works, sees the flash of kingfishers from the colonising willow trees, and on the opposite bank a fisherman casts his lure. In Hailey Park, the end's in sight, the river behind spiked railings. A down-and-out on a bench drags on his cigarette, sips at his Special Brew, contemplates. Another weir's all turbulence and noise, kayakers sporting beneath it, blades of their paddles flashing, red lifejackets bobbing. A colony of young ravens feed and call next to a leafy, suburban avenue. Joggers heave by. Over a traffic-congested bridge, through a meadow and by a shadowy rise I reach the west door of the cathedral. It is sunlit, shining:

> *. . . and how much do you have?*
> *Lisp the bells of Llandaf.*

Inside, sunlight from a clearing sky floods through clear, high windows into the nave and a young priest with a mobile phone at his belt bustles past. All along the north aisle, by the door to the Welsh Regiment Chapel, are tattered flags, battle standards. I drift over to them, look up. An attendant or visitor, well-dressed, upright, elderly, moves close, catches my eye.

'These are the regimental standards,' he explains.

'I see,' I respond, 'and which are the ones for the Argyll and Sutherland Highlanders, the Lancashire Fusiliers, the Royal Munster Fusiliers, the West Riding Regiment?'

'Oh, I don't think they'd be here. More likely to be in their own churches. I could go and ask for you. Would there be a reason for them to be hanging here?'

'They were used to put down the Merthyr radicals in 1831, the Tonypandy miners in 1910. I imagine the Church would have approved.'

'Ah! I see . . .' His eyes look from side to side. 'Most interesting to talk to you. The church isn't the place to provoke discussion or argument, you know. We come here to worship God. Good day.'

I looked up at Sir Jacob Epstein's mesmerically hideous, haunted, aluminium 'Christ in Majesty', suspended from a concrete drum of an organ-case atop twin parabolic pre-cast concrete arches, shook my head and made for the door. Outside in the bright early evening, I walked through Llandaf Fields and into Pontcanna. The wine-bars and the bistros were already filling up, the BMWs sidling into parking spaces between skips outside houses in process of renovation.

We'll quaff wine, we'll eat Manna,
Boast the bells of Pontcanna.

There was running through my head a passage from the Good Tory Disraeli's novel of 1870, *Lothair.* It goes like this:

Two nations; between whom there is no intercourse and no sympathy; who are as ignorant of each other's habits, thoughts, and feelings, as if they were dwellers in different zones, or inhabitants of different planets; who are formed by a different breeding, are fed by a different food, are ordered by different manners, and are not governed by the same laws.

'You speak of –', said Egremont hesitatingly.

'The rich and the poor.'

On a Cardiff pavement on a fine May evening, the wind abated and a warm sun shining down, after days of travelling on foot through the country I know and love best in this world, I found the tears streaming down my cheeks; and blank incomprehension of the past and present, fear of the future and for my children, flooding in on me:

That which is true, the understanding ratifies: that which is good the heart owns: all other claims are spurious, vitiated, mischievous, false.

William Hazlitt

NOTES

[1] Patrick Leigh Fermor, *A Time to Keep Silence* (John Murray, 1957).

[2] Raymond Williams, *Border Country* (Chatto & Windus, 1960).

[3] Ibid.

[4] William Langland, The Vision of William concerning Piers the Plowman (E.E.T.S. 1869).

[5] Michael Foot: *Aneurin Bevan 1897-1945* (MacGibbon & Kee, 1962).

[6] Kenneth O. Morgan, *Rebirth of a Nation: Wales 1880-1980* (O.U.P./ O.W.P. 1982).

[7] Gwyn Alf Williams, *The Merthyr Rising of 1831* (2nd Edition, University of Wales Press, 1988).

[8] William Wordsworth, 'The Old Cumberland Beggar'.

[9] Glyn Jones, *The Dragon Has Two Tongues* (Dent, 1968).

[10] M. Wynn Thomas, *Corresponding Cultures,* (University of Wales Press, 1999).

[11] Anthony Conran, *The Cost of Strangeness* (Gomer, 1982).

[12] Gwalia Deserta XXVI, in *The Collected Poems of Idris Davies* (Gomer, 1972).

[13] Reproduced in Peter Lord's magnificent *The Visual Culture of Wales: Industrial Society* (University of Wales Press, 1998).

[14] 'everything must go' in Patrick Jones, *Fuse* (Parthian Books, 2001).

[15] From Idris Davies's journals, quoted in the introduction to the *Collected Poems.*

ANOTHER WAY

Robert Minhinnick

ANOTHER WAY

'I know another way.'

He would say that, wouldn't he? The thin man. I knew he was going to say that. The moment I'm sure of the route, north and north-west, past the Butcher's Arms in Llandaf, or off the cathedral green, along by the BBC, or maybe across to Whitchurch and the house called Khasia, north and north-west anyway, he has to offer his own alternative. Which of old, I'm sure, will involve roads not marked on any maps, not that the thin man ever consulted a map, not in his own country anyway, roads frost-heaved and rutted by the wheels of hay-wagons and death-carts, roads with burned-out Cavaliers on the corners but always an absence of traffic, roads with armchairs abandoned under oaktrees, roads where buzzards wait like dismal pensioners for the bus that is a century too late, roads that turn west when you're seeking the north, roads that pass farms with ragwort in the beilis, building sites with sycamores seeded in the foundations, roads that double-back so you're surprised you don't meet yourself coming the other way, roads under hedges black with bryony where a green cockscomb grows up the middle, roads so narrow you must walk sideways, roads to places that are no longer places, roads to places only he would know. Yes, he would say that, wouldn't he, the thin man, who is already leading me out of the suburbs, or the villages that became suburbs, good places, expensive places, all gnocchi and nokkias now of course, but in their time part of a vision, a creed that honoured life. *I know another way,* he says. *But we can't start here.*

But start we must. Under the Llandaf cathedral yews. I'm glad they're still here, alive and poisonous. Fifteen years ago I stood under these yews with a television journalist and local MP and talked about what acid rain was doing to the vitals of Wales. Frankly, I predicted doom. And was right in a way. But doom proves itself a cell by cell process. There was no apocalypse. So it's good to talk to the yews again, to acknowledge their reasonable health. Because the yew is a powerful tree. It comes out of the neolithic to us in an immemorial dynasty.

Over its red dust we make our way, across to the Taff. We'll look at the river a while, then follow it north. The Taff's our compass needle. But the thin man needs no compass, he says. And we're travelling without the assistance of the Director General of the Ordnance Survey. What does he know and where has he been? So, not for the last time, let's stray a little.

The Taff in its time was a quilt of iron dust. It was a coal vein broken open to the light. The Taff was once so thick with coal, people claimed its waters looked like funeral crepe. But now the final indignity. They have taken away its tides. So the Taff drowns itself in the teaspoon of the Cardiff Barrage. Back there at Llandaff and now at Taff's Well it flows beside me, coming out of the carboniferous, pushing through the circlet of limestone that rings the coalfield of south Wales on the geological map, the coalfield coloured grey as a tumour, though as a Cardiff poet has told us, tumours might ripen into rose. So here it runs, silver, suicidal. It has otters and trolleys and toilet paper, kingfishers and colliers on its conscience, and of children like Wiffin there's no counting. And at the same time as in Taff's Well it is behind us at Llandaff where in the cathedral Epstein's Christ is squeezing himself out of an enormous toothpaste tube, and simultaneously flowing through Bute Park and into the city's aboretum, and surely of the cities I know it's only Rio has a richer rainforest in its midst, and on to our glass parliament and the Millennium Centre. So let's hear it for the Taff. Let's drown its own aria with an oratorio of our own, then allow the First Minister to offer a valediction as the river slumps into the dock beside him, *Guilty, your Honour, Guilty as Sin*, and its name is dissolved in the Bay's acid bath.

I'm walking north. But in less than a mile the way is blocked. Here's the motorway – a Serengeti for the age of speed. I stand on the M4 bridge below Radyr watching its metronome of life. And such life, a teeming ecology, the prey and the predatory mixed in together. Usually, where there's no going over, I go under. Under at Kenfig to the sand-scoured castle, under at Llewellyn Street where you might lean from the terrace windows and touch the concrete piles, under at the Cymdda where the new Wales has been constructed overnight in the ultra violet of the Odeon and the sacristy of McArthur Glen. And when you stand under the motorway and read the writing on its pillars, when you hear the unrelenting wheels above your head, you know the motorway for what it is: a path of pilgrimage. Because we all commute. The sea twice a day, the call centre Kayleighs, the DIY warehouse Gavins, the planets in rare affiliation in the north-west tonight, which is the direction we're taking. Commuters are the pilgrims today and if there's anything I've learned it's that we are pilgrims or we are nothing. There's white van man, that pilot fish of commerce in the fast lane, because if ever there was a pilgrim it is white van man gunning it to destiny, 90, 95, the orgasmic ton: and there stalled on the hard shoulder, the saleswoman's Focus; and you and I in the hayrattle meadow that is now the Grenada forecourt at Cardiff West, and ten minutes later we can be above the Cymdda where one day the cottongrass and peatwater black as espresso will be restored. Because this is it: our barrier reef. And there's no better place to observe it than this bridge. I suppose I could have dashed across, there are gaps in the traffic, but only the bridge permits this panorama. And what a place to stand. This is our balcony in the eye of the storm as the M4 disappears in its ribbon of platinum dust and the cherryblossom streams into the drains.

With me on the road through Gwaelod y Garth is Edward Lhuyd. We stopped at the pub, although the village hostelry considers itself an inn, and indisputably an inn it is, a stone tavern built from the stone that rises behind it and gives the village its name and purchase. But only for a couple, though already my legs are as heavy as my head is light, and now on the road through the fields our talk is of garlic. My attention at the bar had been drawn by a woman with a bowl of soup. How she sipped, gracefully as an avocet, her upturned spoon its upturned beak, over the gleaming mere. But Lhuyd had been arrested by garlic twiglets. By garlic mayonnaise. By the garlic-flavoured crisps, the scree and swarf scented with garlic in their sealed purses, the iron filings flavoured with garlic in saucers upon the counter, the limestone chews impregnated with garlic, the granite shavings immersed in garlic, the beechwood toast and oaken baguettes overwhelmed by garlic. I had enjoyed our snack, but Lhuyd's teeth are not what they were. I try to stop his complaint. After all, there are bullfinches in the hedge, their breasts so red you'd think them naked, there are buzzards catcalling over the wood, and yes, Lhuyd is right, there is a white road of garlic that follows our road, that bends when it bends, that climbs as we rise. There's no time to stop so we taste as we go. Certainly Lhuyd is right. This is garlic as it should be, this is garlic with the rain on it, wild garlic under its white veil, a wedding trail of garlic in the grass behind us, and here's the ghost of garlic on my fingers, a succulence that won't let go.

Common enough, I say, chewing another leaf.

'*Allium ursinum*,' he says.

'Ramsons,' I say. 'Or is it ransoms. Ransoms is better. As in the poem. Sort of a wild onion. Long may it hold me to ransom.'

'Of the family *Liliaceae*.'

'Well answer me this,' I say. 'Why did we never cook with it? Here it is, free food. A larder a mile long. And no recipes for wild garlic. Not poisonous, is it?'

'Pigs wouldn't eat it.'

'Think,' I say. 'We could have put in in soups. In stews. Cooked meat with it. All that tough mutton. All that bad cheese. It's crying out for ransoms. All that bread that smells like library books.'

'Horses wouldn't look at it.'

'We could sell it,' I say. 'We could bag it up and sell it in Ponty market for a quid a bunch. Make us rich.'

Lhuyd goes quiet. The light, as we climb, devastates. The view grows with every step. But we see only as far as we allow ourselves. There are so many greens you'd need a National Gallery of Green to reproduce them.

'What's that?' I ask, pointing. There's another white flower following us. It's been there a long time. No matter how fast we walk, we can't throw it off.

'Ah,' says Lhuyd. '*Stellaria holostea*. Shirtbutton. In your language, the greater stitchwort. Adder's meat.'

'So we can eat it?'

Lhuyd says nothing.

Eventually we stop at the entrance to a wood. He tells me that the wood is filling like a butt of rainwater almost to the brim. He talks of enchanter's nightshade. He describes dog's mercury. He points to the twaybladed orchid with its undistinguished spire. We walk on. There are bluebells under the sycamores in a reef that stretches as far as I can see.

'On your knees,' says the botanist, and on our knees we breathe the scent. But I prefer looking. Yet looking is dangerous. There is something hallucinatory about bluebells. As I gaze at these flowers I suspect a narcotic in the air, such is their perfume, such is the quality of their blue. I am underwater now and the blue's a balm somehow inside my eyes and I am swimming in its lagoon. Surely these flowers are poisonous. Because soon I'm paralysed. But my mind is walking on, though beside me Lhuyd lies down. This is as far as he goes, he says, for this wood is a bower of quiet for us, and a sleep full of sweet dreams, and health, and quiet breathing.

It's not long before I reach Taff's Well. The village is engulfed by roads. Here's Omega Security, its dogs, its cameras, so many cameras on this route we might make a CCTV movie of ourselves stumbling out of the woods and into the revolution of consumer paranoia. I've been a trespasser all my life, and pilgrim, you should be aware of that if you're following this trail. Under the barbed wire, away from the beaten track; watching for farmers on Suzukis, gamekeepers in Taff-coloured corduroy. Once it was child's play to leave their prosecuting voices behind. But they are the old enemy. It's a new game now and there's less of a future in trespassing as the cameras turn like flowers towards the sun or reveal who stirs in the stonewashed small hours.

But something's barring the way. I've arrived at the sheds of the supermarket, so large they might hold aeroplanes. But this is no factory, and in I go under the cameras that caress all who enter, and at once with who knows what avatastic instinct, I find I've adopted the sleepwalkers' demeanour necessary to prove myself a supplicant of the store.

Half a mile away is Castell Coch. Which is where you might be now, rapping on the portcullis, imagining Lady Bute stepping out of her chemise as she looks down at the treetops from her bedchamber. But if you've followed me you'll see I'm pricing Leeward Island bananas, figs from Greece. Then considering energy drinks that Fed-ex caffeine to the blood, proteins that restore hope, vitamins that recover determination. I'm down one aisle and up the next, eyes left, eyes right. We need it all, we need the world, its sunflower seeds rattling in my basket, the staff of fair trade chocolate to help me over what's to come. Now I'm searching for something to feed the imagination. Starfruit? Pecarino or Paracetamol? Maybe pumpernickel, wheatgerm, or the phials of the detox shelves. Or lollo rosso, groundnuts, evening primrose. What about enchiladas, gewurztraminer, zinfandel? Perhaps chilli dog, happy dog, slush, crush, the original Neapolitan peasant recipe with extra olives, because we're all ravenous in the land of plenty, lost in the supermarket's garden of forking paths.

It's not Castell Coch. But we might as well enjoy it. The place is big as a small town. At every hour it boasts such a town's population. This is a high street under striplights and people are here because other people are here and there's gossip and glamour and only for the dwindling few the memory of what existed before this place was built, the voices under the ground, the shiggling lamps, the blackpats. Soon, life before the supermarket will be an inconceivable past. And then, when it is sufficiently strange, when it is irrecoverable, we will make films about it and statues will be raised and historians will give judgement and the rest of us will shrug and think there but for the grace of God goes . . . but Lady Bute at the checkout is asking if I need cashback. Look, pilgrim, here's a miracle indeed. I'm leaving with fifty more than when I came in. Happy dog.

Immediately I stand in a predicament of roads. The straightest route is around Taff's Well and north between ash trees whose black buds have yet to unfurl and more of those shirtbuttons rolling in the grass. This week I met the poet, Landeg White, who left Taff's Well aged five and has not returned. Until now. I am reading his book, *Traveller's Palm*, which reeks of his time in Africa, of its maize porridge and prison cells, and of his Portuguese home with its carafes of green wine. No-one in Taff's Well remembers Landeg White. No-one in Wales remembers him. The poet made the mistake of becoming exotic. But now the son has returned. Ah well, I shrug, and turn aside from the road.

Instead I retreat towards the Garth. Up, over, and here is Efail Isaf and not a soul to be seen in the village. In a garden I watch a sparrowhawk alight. It seizes a young blackbird. Soon around the hawk is a circle of feathers. Outside that circle is a circle of silence where nothing can intrude. Outside that second circle is a circle of uncertain silence. And outside that circle is the grief of the cock bird's voice. It approaches the hawk as closely as it dares. But the two circles of silence are forbidden to it. It watches as its chick is torn apart and devoured. Then the hawk rises and takes a second. Looking around the lawn, it makes the killing with its spur, calm at the centre of the circles where the rite is performed. Soon there are two circles of feathers, each with two circles of silence around them. The world is forbidden to enter those circles. The blackbird is forbidden and I know I am forbidden. No creature, no magic or sacrifice can alter the power of those circles. They were drawn before we discovered the purpose of our minds.

When the hawk flies off the circles disappear and soon there's cuckoo spit on my legs and the pennants of lords-and-ladies beginning to thrust aside the litter; snake berries we used to call them, and here's a field full of milkmaids close to white-painted St. Illtud's at Upper Church Village and you might look a long time for milkmaids in the dictionaries and come away disappointed, but this is my childhood around me, smoking out of the dew, pollen poltergeists moving ahead and behind, and I can put a face and a name to every one of those ghosts, for these are my traveller's palms and at this instant it seems impossible to believe that anything lost will not eventually be returned.

Footsore, I'm in the lanes. There's a whirlpool of trails around here. I know a better way, said the thin man, but we're going west when I know east of Mynydd y Glyn is called for. There are S bends and empty roadsigns and if this is the way to Pontypridd it is the route I would take in a post-apocalypse Wales when all identities have vanished and there's no right and wrong. Here at a crossroads is another hollow sign, and tied to barbed wire is a cellophane bouquet. Someone must have died in this place. Somebody lost or travelling too fast, eager to leave this country that has no name. What should be happening now is our descent into Graig, dangerous for pedestrians, and our triumphant arrival in Taff Street. But I travel with a companion who thinks he knows a better way and soon there's a notice on a wall that confirms my suspicions. 'Pant y Brad' it says. Even I know that *brad* means treachery, and if you've been fool enough to

follow us you will have already understood that something underhand is going on. Because if this is Pant y Brad we have come south-west of the Rhondda Fawr. If this is Pant y Brad I've betrayed my own instincts. It means our road now must lead to Tonyrefail, dreary Ton that must have something going for it, and, be my guest, traveller, discover what's hidden here. Then up to Trebanog and the man with a pitbull guarding the entrance to the Rhondda. Cerberus is straining at both leash and belly-belt and its handler follows with his own pitbull's gait, the dog wheezing, the man in a white singlet pulling it back into the Rhiwgarn estates where I consider it unnecessary to follow, Rhiwgarn being Rhiwgarn.

Not that Taff Street's Easy Street. In its day it knew tumultuous trade and maybe there are reminders of that past for those who know where to look. But the Queen of the Valleys is on librium now, and as you see, here's more *brad*. I've doubled back, gone down the Graig, and find myself peering into the window of Mid Glamorgan Goldsmiths. Who must be pleased with themselves. Young Ponty men have adopted the fashions of The Bronx and East New York. They drip with chains and bracelets, their knuckles are fat with signet rings as they reach for their phone top-up cards. See them best on the Friday night parade between the Market Tavern and Angharad's, and the Ponty girls too in clingy gangs, crop-topped and pale-bellied, shivering like eels come out of the stream.

The town looks exactly what it is. A place from which certainty has ebbed. The traditional life choices have vanished: men in the pit, the women at home or stitching underwear in the Rhondda, and on a Saturday night a visit to the Town Hall for 'Billy Maxman the Wonder Fool' followed by 'Yeamans' Famous Footballing Dogs'. But maybe that's naive. Pontypridd was always the most middle class of valley towns. I used to teach evening classes at Coed y Lan and remember substantial villas with evergreen gardens overlooking the terraces. And there have always been money and elegance as well as radical politics in Graigwen.

But Queen of the Valleys? It's a republican age. What Ponty cries out for is exploration of its teeming history and problematical present by artists and writers. No town deserves it more. Alun Richards is Ponty's most famous literary son, while John L. Hughes's *Tom Jones Slept Here* is worth searching for in second-hand book shops. But it's a rant. And that maybe is the curse of younger English language 'valley writers': their anger. We hear the voice of the victim and the victim usually conforms to stereotype. What we need is an urban lyricist with a pathologist's eye (but not a pathologist's mind); a bedsitter scientist who can interpret the genome of contemporary English. And if that sounds romantic, all well and good. Real writers are always romantics but rarely admit to it. Because to write today in Pontypridd is an exhilarating romantic act. But as to anger, choose it, use it, but get over it. Anger was never the most innovative search-engine of the writer's imagination.

Pilgrims grow thirsty. By chance, here is the Trehafod Hotel. It's ten years since I stood in the public bar and I'm trying to understand what's changed. Nothing, it seems. Nothing apart from everything. Because I'm a new man. Since I last stood here every cell in my body has died and been reborn. The carbon is new, the hydrogen is new. Like those Hopkinstown homies I'm priceless with new gold. Maybe minds too are reborn. Perhaps there is a renaissance of the imagination. Then why does the spirit fail? Why do we give up the ghost if the ghost too is a new ghost? Before me the atoms of the mirror are dead atoms. The uptipped double litre of London Dry with its juniper garland will never undergo rebirth. And there are my greyed hairs in that mirror that were never there before, while my thoughts conspiring now around the gin were not previously concerned with time. Time? It's massing around me like Mynydd y Glyn, there to the west. It's building itself in the east like The Glôg. And squeezing me into it, another fossil in its cliff. Now The Glôg I can stand. And maybe Mynydd y Glyn I might negotiate. But I know what's coming. Cefn Craig Amos, that's what's coming. Pilgrim, that's a brutal ridge. There'll be no shrugging off Cefn Craig Amos, no optimism about scaling that precipice. But that's the future. That's the end of this journey. And what's ten years? A moment. So make your tribute to the god of thirst here in the Trehafod Hotel. And think of the moments of which The Glôg is built.

The pilgrimage progresses even as we rest. And soon you will notice that the Trehafod Hotel is no place for the pious. There are pieties here innumerable, but the pious should beware. And now it arrives. Your drink. The drink you have ordered but which in another reality has been ordered for you. It's been waiting a long time.

There is always something numinous about a pint come over the bar. Forget what it costs and ignore its antecedence. It will taste like the Taff yet reassemble your perceptions of self. It will instill holiness before the paranoia starts, but life is impossible without the delusions your glass will bring to you. In Llandaf in the Butcher's you might sit under the Brain's diamond in your own blue diamond of smoke and know that the path taken is no more crooked than the path to come. In Graigwen at the Tŷ Mawr the regulars will know you for a pilgrim before you have carried your glass to your seat and they will understand entirely that pilgrimage but not easily illustrate their understanding. And at The Rickyard Arms coming down the hill towards Porth and its bazaar selling Queen Elizabeth Golden Jubilee street party union jacks (discount) we might stand Gwyn Thomas a drink. But choose a seat near the door. Exits are important to Gwyn.

Less garrulous than of old, he has his opinions.

'What's become of the Rhondda, Gwyn?'

'What indeed?'

'Who are these inheritors, Gwyn, in their NY ballcaps and Adidas gear? In their white trainers with shock absorbers in the toes? No, steelies now, Gwyn. Their feet are soft.'

'NY?' he asks. 'Ah, yes. *Not Yours.*'

'So who are these Rhondda men, Gwyn, heads shaved, faces ringed and pierced?'

'The sons of their fathers,' the maestro breathes, over his American cream soda. 'No more, no less. But don't ask me what they do. Work has changed.'

And he thinks a moment. 'Do people work these days? I know they're busy. Sometimes I watch the boys when their phones ring. That instant of bliss. Somebody's calling. Somebody cares. And there's me,' he says, taking a first sip, 'who hasn't had a telephone call since 1981.'

'Mr Thomas,' I say, 'tell me one thing before you go. I've always wanted to know why people planted monkey puzzle trees in the Rhondda.'

'Ah! Our great conundrum,' he says. 'I've counted them all. And each is a friend. A little misplaced, aren't they, but brave. It's their bravery I admire. And the pretension too. Which is always one thing we lacked. Pretension. How we were warned against it. That was our great virtue, see. Our unpretentiousness. But sometimes people make vices out of their virtues . . .'

And then he has to borrow a handkerchief because the cream soda bubbles have gone up his nose.

But as in The Rickyard, two miles closer to where we are heading today, or two miles further away, as Mr Thomas put it before slipping out, so here in the Trehafod: a word of advice. Be wary of the landlord's expression. Vacancy and animation are masks. Both angels and demons are found behind public-house counters and I have been obliged by both. The deranged inhabit these places. The deranged are people who do not share your derangement. The stupid too are found in here. The stupid are those who do not acknowledge your wisdom. There will be cowards also, who will not credit your courage. Above all, admit the ritual. The nun with her Bristol Cream, the murderer with his low-cal, have sat where you sit now. Under the window in a torrent of spring light. Thirst is our dangerous blessing. And, as I say, there is always something numinous in a glass that is passed across the bar. As if that glass were a pilgrimage's reward and the pilgrim's absolution. So, drink up. But know that glass for either a piety or an enchantment. They are similar conditions. Which is something you should not ponder too long at the Trehafod Hotel.

We're now either ahead of ourselves or behind. But don't worry. We're all going to the same place. And Trehafod is instructional for those attuned to the lessons of history. Here's what's left of Lewis Merthyr colliery, but unlike the hundreds of other coal mines in the valley, it has not been grassed over or turned into a superstore. It's now the site of the Rhondda Heritage Park, dedicated to mining. A brief visit will confirm two suspicions. First, winning coal was a terrible trade. Second, existentialism never made it to the coalfield. The miners were heroes, but obedient heroes, as their wives were heroic and obedient in their turn. And together, men and women mined the inexhaustible seam of their own loyalty. Even as the walls collapsed, even as their children were scalded to death or were wasted by rickets and diptheria, even as the money haemorrhaged south into the starry boudoirs of Castell Coch and on to the Mount Stuart banks where the world's first cheque for a million pounds was penned, they remained paragons of obedience. Instructional, traveller? Oh yes, at Trehafod we might learn a good deal about ourselves.

But whose heritage is this? Mine, indupitably. Who was never down a pit in his life. Who will always refuse any invitation to the memorial shafts. So at Trehafod I visit the fan engine house. Of all colliery equipment, the fan engine was the most important. Here, I think of the draughts the engines blew underground and imagine those purifying blasts travelling through darkness on the way to the lungs of the thousands who cut the coal and filled the drams. Of fresh air invading the colonnades and the dead ends, its incense chilling the skin; fresh air from the censors of the fan engines blowing down the coal roads, fresh air lengthening the sentences of those already condemned.

Coal.

I distrust that word. What does it imply but subterranean suffocation? Working class claustrophobia? A culture with the roof fallen in? At Trehafod fragments of a forgotten language are pieced together, an effort is made to understand a cataclysm. But it's rarely like this in the coalfield. So come again away from our route although our journey is as much about time as it is about topography, and here I am at the HQ gate of National Coal Board Area Number 2 and escorting my mother around the ruins.

Not that there are ruins to see. We're not into ruins any more. But at Area Number 2 there's not a sign to tell the visitor what this place meant to the world. There's not a plaque, not a brick upon another brick to indicate how this *nothingness* in its time controlled the lives of hundreds of thousands of people. Only a gate that leads to a wood of spectral buddleia. The offices where my mother typed her coal chores on a ribboned Remington, where she looked up and saw for the first time that thin man, the soldier from Rangoon, my father, at his own coal chores, are demolished. Sacked. If you want to see a masterpiece of demolition, the sacrilege of sackage, go to Area Number 2. There's nothing there. Only a woman left to paint the air and hear the Remingtons ring.

But back then, everything was coal. The Fourteenth Army had returned from Burma, the emaciated subalterns and skin-and-bone corporals of the Welch Regiment were trying to fashion a life after Tungoo, after Mawchi. And demobbed legions, which included my father, entered the byzantium of coal that was Area Number 2.

Three hundred million years ago when Wales lay on the equator God decreed that this part of the world should one day provide coal. The geology was inescapable Because geology is totalitarian no-one argued with it. With everything else we could have bent the rules: invoked character, nature, even genetics. But we couldn't argue with geology. Or with another geological force, Margaret Thatcher, when she decreed coal must cease. But Thatcher's proclamation came too late for me. I was already made. Made by coal. Coal made me when my mother looked up from her typewriter. Coal made me when my father, malarial, too small for his suit, a secondhand Meakers of Piccadilly in West of England wools, followed the buyers down the National Coal Board corridor and into the typing pool. So there's coal in my blood. There's coal in my bones. I never think about it, but surely my heart is made of coal.

And now here are two of us on our visit to nowhere. The gate opens, the buddleias drip rain, and there's a rain-washed nothing where the area HQ used to be. A site of grim pillage. Two of us today, but I think of my father amongst the tree-ferns, sipping from pitcherplants, macheteing the mangroves. In three hundred million years there will be coal measures in Burma. In Myanma. God is decreeing it as I write. And there's no argument about that. No war can be fought to stop geology happening. Freedom fighters cannot win against geology. The Generals of Myanma cannot place geology under house arrest. Not even the Fourteenth Army, not even the Welch Regiment with its muletrains and genial headhunters scouting the way could defeat geology.

But at least my father had medals. Not that he kept them. Down the road in the munitions factory the girls turned yellow. They didn't have medals. They went to the Palais de Danse and the Grand Pavilion in their yellow nylons of dynamite dust, the unseasonal tans, the saffron face-powder. But no-one gave them medals. No wonder they went through the roof.

No-one gave the colliers any medals either. At the time. But how we've made up for it since. Now we award the miners literature's sympathy medals, art's nostalgia medals, the sentimental medals pinned on by politicians, by historians, by children who'll never need to squeeze themselves into the coffin-deep seam of Garth Ton Mawr or Pen Llwyn Gwent or any other mine.

So what am I doing here? Here at the gate in the afternoon downpour. Asking for a medal of course. For a medal on the gate because there's nowhere else to put it now. A medal that records what has vanished. What has vanished as utterly as the tree-ferns and equatorial orchids that flourished where the buddleia now drips its rain. Because you cannot argue with geology. Or with the new geology. Because there's a new geology now. It's a speeded-up geology. Three hundred million years in three hundred million seconds. It's that stratum of amnesia that's building itself, a buddleia leaf here, a memorial stanza there, between the now and the what's-to-come. That's the new geology. Open the gate at Area Number 2, off the Maesteg Road, in the village of Tondu, in the country of Wales, and watch its black seam laying itself implacably, totalitarianally, down.

There's no amnesia at Trehafod. But even here, or especially here, when I try to think of the coalfield, that tumour intrudes. The tumour on the map. Maybe I was a fool to hang it on my wall, that map of an unpeopled Wales, the map of the arbitrary grains beneath our feet: a free Wales indeed of mudstone and volcanoes and the physics of rock, a pre-cambrian Wales, a pre-Wales Wales. I pass them every day, those western peninsulas with their psychedelic geology, on my commute from study to kitchen. Then there is the limestone of north and south, and a pagan rainbow in the east: the witch country around Church Stretton. And last the coalfield painted in grey and etched with a forest of faults.

The pits are closed but coal cannot be escaped. I walk on the southern beaches every afternoon and find coal mingled with the sand. There's a seam that runs a mile under the sea near where I live. The old Newlands pit was worked for decades, so clean was that coal, the miners curling themselves like tribolites into the seabed, taking light and language and their own hot blood into places where they didn't belong, into places where no life belongs unless it is blind and cold and unnameable. And on those beaches I hear the fairground, the cries from the SkyMaster, the Ghost Train, and yes, the coalfield will always be a ghost train to me, a ghost train shuttered for the night and the winter, but where as if in a dream I am leased to wander on a winter night through its corridors, passing the faces of legend in their shrines, the dead and the undead, the eyes, the mouths, the victims, the victorious, all fossils together in those dungeons, and every passage indistinguishable from the last.

And if it's a labyrinth there is only one guide who can take us through. Because if the coalfield is a labyrinth only Jorge Luis Borges knows the way out. Yes, maybe that's how I see the coalfield now. A labyrinth with a dead minotaur. A labyrinthine library whose books are fossils. A library of Babel where everything is written but nothing is read. Yes, let Borges take us through, and let us search with him for the last miner, the lost miner whom only Borges can find in these circular ruins, because only a Borges can bring back our Taff Steet Theseus who has let go the thread, but who still clutches his snap, his lamp, his vocabulary of extinct trades, and who hews at the rock every day beneath our feet.

'Could have come in from there,' gestures the thin man, waving at the east and the Rhondda Fach. 'Over the mountains from Llanwonno.'

I know the road. It comes through a forest, melancholy at the best of times. But it's drama he describes. Because there's drama at every entry to these valleys. You have to fight to get into the Rhondda. You have to want to be there. Whether it's over Bwlch y Clawdd to the west, the Rhigos and Llethr Las to the north, or scowling Trebanog where the mastiff lurks, it's what a pilgrimage should be. I know another way, said the thin man, and now we're looking down over the momentous vale. There are the roofs of the Rhondda Fawr, and when we turn there is the waste tip that is coal's sarcophagous, the colour and shape of Silbury Hill.

'I used to know its name', he says. In this light there's a sinister geometry to the tip. I shake my head.

We had come through Wattstown and Ynyshir, then taken the hill. Now on Penrhys we stare and listen to the dogs. There's no chance of

refreshment. At the top of the estate we call at the Pendyrus RAOB Social Club but the doors are barred. Above us are the conifers but this is as high as we get. A burned-out bus shelter; the black satellites like wreaths. There's a cry in Heol Teifionydd, a whisper in Heol Pendyrus. And then a silence. Somehow here we are out of the world. We passed a boundary somewhere or blundered through a forcefield and now stand beyond what's familiar. Children are playing in a puddle, there's washing on the lines, but it's clear we've crossed a frontier. It's a different world and I don't belong. Traveller, may it be otherwise for you. All I know is that Penrhys was designed like a village overlooking the Tyrrhenian sea, yet often the wind that blows here feels as if it has crossed Iceland. And that when the locals stare at me I cannot meet their eyes. Yes, this is as high as I will ever reach above the Virgin on her lawn.

I look at the statue. It's a glum and bone-coloured Mary we find, this virgin of the oaks. Nearby are ruined chapel walls where once the medieval poor came to worship. Visitors should bring their own exultancy to this place. They will find little here. If their Welsh is good enough, they'll learn that the original statue was destroyed – *dinistriwyd*, such an emphatic word – on September 26, 1538. This replacement was erected in 1953. A little nun from Porthcawl, brown as a fieldfare, was one of those who suggested the restoration of the shrine. She took a party of schoolgirls up the windy hill. One of the pupils walked with a leg-iron. The other girls waited for the miracle. John Newman in his *Buildings of Glamorgan* wrote that the statue would seem to belong 'in Ecuador'. With which we should all disagree. Exquisite it is not, but its creators should be allowed their bold design. How well we've been trained to ridicule the pretentious. *Remember the monkey puzzle*, hisses a ghost.

We're finished here. And begin again. I leave the valley by another way, the road north into Ferndale and on to Maerdy. Poor Maerdy. Little Moscow they used to call it, and now they don't call it very much at all, this part of the Rhondda Fach being somewhat on its uppers, and there's North Terrace which is where the Rhondda ends, and there is Institute Street where its ghost laments. Because here is the sad baroque of the Institute itself, one of the great remaining buildings of this world, a library, a theatre, and a statement made by workers' pennies if ever such a statement was made, and if you come this way remember it was the thin man who suggested it, and note the lesson of Pant y Brad, but if you still decide to take this road, push open the Institute's metal doors and step inside. Then gaze at what remains of generations of self-sacrifice. This will happen under the shadow of Cefn Craig Amos. I promised you that ridge and here it is: a bulwark that hides the sun and chills the waters of the Rhondda Fach. There's a school built in its shadow. No place for a school, I think, looking at the unremitting rock, thinking of the classrooms dark in the morning and those cliffs shuttering their glass. But already we are leaving it behind. We're going beyond.

Because what are any of us if not pilgrims? For me, at least, that's an attractive thought. An explanatory thought. It clarifies a good deal about my life. Whether in the museum or Gwaelod's limestone maw or the slumland shrine of Penrhys, all of us pursue a sacred commute: white van-man, Kayleigh from the Call Centre, and the *crachach* of the Beeb breathing into their Samsungs. And remember that the Taff, first pilgrim to be encountered in the hereabouts of this essay, on the way to an ignominious end, must begin somewhere out of our reckoning in a droplet no bigger than a grain of rice.

ALONG THE RIDGES

Patrick Dobbs

ALONG THE RIDGES

All men should strive, before they die,
to find what they're running from,
and to, and why.

James Thurber,
Further Fables For Our Time

My pilgrimage begins at Penrhys, high above the confluence of Rhondda Fach and Rhondda Fawr. I stand beside a larger than life statue of the Virgin Mary, an unexpected monument in the heart of the coalfield which has an all-pervasive democratic socialist tradition that owes more to Methodism than to Marx, and next to nothing to Mary.

At her feet is a holy well, but her gaze is eternally focussed across Llwynypia and Tonypandy in the valley below. The infant saviour, inspiration of two thousand years, nestles to her breast. Between them they stand above the tumult, the squalor, the glory and pain of the two Welsh valleys that have come to be a metaphor for a certain civilization, a culture born of hardship and struggle, a political philosophy founded on a common purpose and united towards a common but always evasive utopia, where labour will have its full reward and everyone will share equally in the wealth of the world.

The stony indifference of virgin and child to the hustle and bustle of their surroundings is neither haughty nor condescending; rather it is contented, compassionate and forbearing. Over Mary's left shoulder is the tamed, truncated, but still vast tump of Wattstown colliery tip, and beyond that the bright green fields of some clearly cherished and well-managed farm. On the mountain ridge a cairn of stones, already very old when the virgin's child was very young. They too in their day surely inspired generations of which we know nothing. Who put them there, and why did they come to these mountain fastnesses where even now the landscape is wild, barren, raw and precipitous?

The story of today's Rhondda Valleys began not hundreds or thousands but millions of years ago, when the outer crust of the earth itself rose and shattered, exposing an outcrop of coal between the overlying measures and the Carboniferous limestone beneath which is all but visible underfoot. The mountain springs carved deep runnels in the rock, the acid eating into the alkali to cut the deep, narrow steep-sided valleys which still isolate one community from another by precipitous mountain passes over barren and inhospitable crags, windswept, often cloud-covered and very wet, with nearly a hundred inches of rain lashing down each year and every year.

Certain figures become archetypal of a certain stage in the story of their place and time: the gun-toting horseman of the western plains of America with his basic sense of right and wrong born out of shared hardship and family necessity; the Roman Legionary with his fierce discipline and messianic sense of order and authority; Renaissance man who saw learning and enlightenment as the path to liberation. So the coalminer, who has stamped this place with his unique and apparently indestructible character, has become a symbol of the workers, a distinct breed of people to be feared, courted, disliked and distrusted by metropolitan man. Feared because the miners were always potentially disruptive of the established social economic and political order; courted because it was necessary to keep them reasonably content if the lights were to stay on and city and suburban life to remain cosy and comfortable; disliked because they had values of their own that were not shared by those that depended on them and distrusted because they were believed to have power without responsibility.

This improbable, awesome and challenging place, in the world but somehow out of this world, has been a refuge, a sanctuary and an inspiration for the saintly, the reclusive and the contemplative since our earliest encounters with gods. St Paulinus, or one of the several of his name, almost certainly climbed up the hill we now call Penrhys fifteen hundred years ago. Six hundred years later the Cistercian Order, whose rule ran 'Our houses shall not be built near cities, castles or villages but in places far removed from the concourse of men', came here to establish a community in 1205 which became the boundary between their great Abbeys of Llantarnam and Margam. But there is evidence that the Bronze age people, so much more civilized than the men of iron that followed them, also recognized this high spur that divides the two valleys as a sacred site. In their day the oak, the elm and the alders were said to be so thick that a squirrel could jump from tree to tree all the way from Pontypridd to Treherbert without putting a paw to the ground, although it would be unlikely to be the same squirrel that is reputed to have performed the same feat from Plynlumon to Eryri.

Different records record different stories, but it is certain that by the fourteenth century Penrhys had become a popular place of pilgrimage, and gifts were piled around the shrine. Sadly for the monks of those days, by the beginning of the fifteenth century the English wool merchants were using their monopoly position in the market to depress the price of Welsh wool. Sheep farming fell on hard times and the monks had to depend on the charity of neighbours. As a flockmaster myself I understand their predicament.

In 1405 Owain Glyndŵr came to this spot to enjoy an eisteddfod after rampaging through South Wales with fire and the sword. He was certainly not the last terrorist thug to seek the consolation of his culture and the blessing of the religious, and both Franciscans and Cistercians backed his cause. Eight years later King Henry V, to teach the monks a lesson, forbade further eisteddfodau at Penrhys, but the ban was lifted by his successor Henry V1 in 1415. The treasures of old Penrhys were finally pillaged by Cromwell's men in 1538. Bishop Latimer wrote to him on the 13th June of that year suggesting a bonfire would 'avoid idolatry', and this final sacrilege was implemented in the front garden of the Lord Protectors' own London residence in Chelsea.

A trickle of pilgrims continued to call over the years both before and after the statue was replaced in 1953. My own arrival, on a cold bright March morning, was preceded by bad omens. I had a couple of warnings not to leave my vehicle unattended, with one more reassuring: 'You probably won't be worth mugging in the clothes you're wearing, mate.' Penrhys has become the archetypal sink estate, where all the bad lots were sent so the drug takers, vandals, graffiti artists, petty and not so petty criminals can feed off each other. The Virgin Mary is all the time looking the other way, unless she has eyes in the back of her head.

I can confirm that the gas men call in pairs, one to watch over their motors while the other does the work, but I have been in far worse places in times past and as you get older you have that much less to lose. The inadequates, the addicts, the dealers, the alcoholics, the misfits and no-hopers of Penrhys were not going to blight my pilgrimage. As I walked along the crescent perimeter road the younger toughs of the place gathered around the remains of a very crashed motor-car wrapped around a miraculously still vertical lamp post. A case, I would have thought, for salvage rather than repair. In fact the bulldozers had been busy demolishing the houses, which ironically were originally designed to form a centre of excellence and gracious living, but are now an eyesore and soon to be nothing but a memory.

A few strides took me away from all sight of tarmacadam and concrete into the woods that cap the Southern spur of Cefn Rhondda, dividing Rhondda Fach from Rhondda Fawr. I could see nothing but the path in front and trees, although the noise of road traffic, motorcycles and what I guessed was clay-pigeon shooting disturbed the tranquillity of Sunday morning. Within yards I stumbled on an old railway line, relic of a mining enterprise of long ago, and some bits of discarded engines, car bodies, mattresses and a refrigerator which was obviously too much trouble to take to a tip.

I walked north and west along an old stone road which was once a highway. The main roads of today, now deep in the valleys, are no more than a hundred and fifty years old. Our ancestors went along the ridges, where I walk now with only the lark and snipe for company, for I met no pedestrians until I was well on my way towards the Neath Valley at Rhigos. Life has changed quickly since miners walked over the top from Aberdare for a day's work in the pit at Ferndale, which I could already see half a mile off but way beneath me, and then walk back home at the end of a hard shift. Very few people seem to walk about nowadays, except on a recreational hike or to cover the very shortest of distances.

Although coal was collected and burnt here back in the sixteenth and seventeenth centuries it was only dug from shallow pits or excavated from exposed seams or levels. The old farmers were churchmen, and Ystradyfodwg vestry book shows that in 1778 coal was bought for heating at fourpence a load. Oxen tilled the fields, and burnt lime was the only inorganic fertilizer.

South Wales was a metal economy before it was a coal economy, and until the nineteenth century commercial mining was undertaken to supply the iron works rather than steam engines, ships or households. When Ferndale tip was sunk in 1862 there were about 4,000 people living in the Rhondda Valleys, and sixty years later there were 163,000 of them. The valleys grew into long thin towns, sometimes described as linear cities. The farms became irrelevant to most people's lives and such farmers as owned their own holdings grew rich not from livestock or crops but from coal. Mass immigration produced a new industrial class, with a completely revolutionary way of looking at the world about them and their place within it. But less than a hundred years later Ferndale pit was done. It saw the disasters of 1869 and '76, the tumultuous battles between the radical socialists of the Communist Party and the reforming faith of the mainstream labour movement and the rise of the Chapels at the expense of the Church. All its personalities and characters, movements and crusades seem as irrelevant now as the Wars of the Roses.

I walked along the ridge in unseasonable sunshine, and saw red-ruffed Glamorgan sheep grazing above Ystrad or Ton Pentre on pastures that had been closed off and sweetened with lime from the quarries beyond Penderyn. The monks of Penrhys would have warmed to the sight of them, well kept, well fed and well cared for. The mountain road became a track of rutted peat, and I soon realised that the whine of the motorcyclists was getting closer. Suddenly a posse of them swooped down from a rocky crest, perhaps a dozen, hard men in helmets and leathers, with their visors down. They paid me no attention whatsoever as they churned by, fully occupied with the task in hand of keeping their machines upright and mobile over tussocky marsh, through pool and pasture.

The A4233 rose from the valley to my right and snaked its blue-grey way over the forested top of Bryn Du towards the further valley and Aberdare. Mardy, home base of novelist and political activist Lewis Jones whose 1930s classic *Cwmardy* became required reading for followers of the Militant tendency fifty years later, was far below me, squeezed between the mountains, the tip and the river.

This is not my country. My forefathers too came from a coal mining

place, not here but set amongst the green fields and rounded hills of County Kilkenny. But there the struggle of the exploited for their place in the sun took a different path altogether, not the road of socialism through the ballot box but nationalism and the gun, not the do-it-yourself religion of Protestant Nonconformity but a powerful and hierarchical and even more authoritarian but somewhat more forgiving Church. Though the politics were different the passions were similar, and to the establishment that depended on them the miners were quite as subversive. When the Castlecomer Board of Guardians was asked for a donation by the Gaelic Athletic Association it was refused on the grounds that they were 'plotting revolution with their hurley sticks', and a grant towards University College, Dublin, was refused for a similar reason. But the isms of yesterday became the wasms of today, and socialism is not so much a God that failed or a philosophy that has never been tried as a promise that was never fulfilled.

To quote Harold Wilson, 'Socialism is a crusade or it is nothing'. In 1910 most Rhondda councillors were middle class liberals, but in 1912 Labour members, coalminers to a man, had completely taken control. In 1999 they lost out to Plaid Cymru and a few independents, and the crusade was over. With their National struggle won the colliers of Castlecomer too are as redundant as the colliers of Treorchy, where only the Russian name remains to remind us of the new dawn that never came.

Looking back in the direction from which I had come I could see the salt water of the Bristol Channel and the hills of Somerset. In the narrow space between the Rhondda Fach and the main road there was just sufficient flat space for a rugby pitch. With so little level ground and so much rain small wonder that rugby, not cricket, is the principal sporting pastime of the valleys.

The mountain tops were studded with wireless masts, from whose sinister surveillance there is no escape. Then I was amongst trees again, unnatural lines of Norway spruce, some blackened by fire, and resin-scented larch already tinged with the red of springtime. I followed a forestry track and once again stumbled upon the culture of abandoned cars, one burnt-out wreck after another, rusting shells that had once stood proud and polished in a dealer's showroom.

Beside the settlement of Mardy the roofs of vast sheds. They shelter the enterprises that have been brought in to replace the jobs lost by redundant miners and their families. How hard these communities have struggled to remain alive! What plant and machinery grants, loans, interest relief, tax allowances, retraining costs and work subsidies have been offered to bribe itinerant investors to set up businesses in the Rhondda! Yet still nearly half the local people leave the valleys to find work. We are a compassionate nation, and have no truck with the ghost towns of the Americas, where company towns, plantations and mines are simply left to disappear into the wilderness once their purpose is exhausted. And yet in our own individual lives we are learning to face the inevitable: when our time comes we switch off the life support machines and let go.

Now there is no natural soil beneath my feet. The distant view is hidden by a prodigious pile of the grey slakey coal and shale of colliery waste. I stand on it and walk on it. It is everywhere. With all the coal that has been carted away, and all this rubbish that has been brought to the surface, the ground beneath must be no more than the cancellar bones of the earth's crust. A brave larch and the occasional stunted spruce, with the scantiest smattering of moor grass and sedge, are all that grow in this heap of useless dirt. Here and there the odd culvert, now mostly broken, and a concrete channel has been set into the shifty slag. They are assumed to be sufficient to stop the whole heap washing down the mountainside on to the houses below.

As every American, and many others world-wide including myself, knows where they were and what they were doing when President Kennedy was shot, so everyone in Wales remembers the sliding tip of Aberfan. On the day of that last awful mass mining disaster in Wales I was buying ponies in Llandovery fair. The gypsies and itinerant horse-dealers, the farmers, the hauliers and the hangers-on dipped into their pockets in what they knew was the futile gesture of a collection for the bereaved. It was all we could do. Auctioneer Vincent Morgan captured the mood, 'Here we are, haggling over the price of a child's pony, but what about those other children? Where are they now?'

Mardy tip was being put to good use that Sunday morning. Some kind of cross-country motorcycle trial was going on, with Marshals,

Timekeepers, Stewards and Judges. They raced up and down and round and round, their bikes jumped high in the air as they revved and roared and splattered me with grey slurry as they went by. Some gave me a cheery wave and surely a grin beneath the anonymity of their helmets.

Near the top of the tip, pockets of snow lingered among the debris of a pile of bulldozed buildings. Great slabs of concrete jagged out into the sky, while four sad crows perched wearily on the rusted reinforcing rods that held the whole mess together.

Now natural ground again, and I could pick out the track from the lie of the land as it continued North towards the Rhigos escarpment. This was an old road, a very old road, that had worn its own bed into the hillside. There was a remnant of an earthen dyke on each side of it. Among the slag heaps and mines you come across ancient castle mounds and rocky cairns whose antiquity is measured not in decades or centuries but in millenia. A haphazard mix in time from current affairs through the more recent past and back to the very beginnings of human society.

I was lost. It was obvious to me that I should follow the contour into the vast coniferous plantation straight ahead of me. I crossed a marsh by leaping from tussock to tussock and stumbled forward towards a patch of drier ground enclosed by an electric fence. Here I am at an advantage over other pilgrims, for as a stock farmer I know how to negotiate electric fencing, even with a sound 240 volt mains connection. Within minutes I had slipped over a line of sheep netting and barbed wire and was making my way north along a convenient fire break. This forest, like so many in Wales, has been planted with scant regard for the established network of footways and horsetracks.

I followed a forestry road which took me above the Lluest Wen reservoir. Once again I was buzzed by recreational motorcyclists, now more elderly and informal, with flowing locks of thinning hair unprotected by any crash helmet. The track was disfigured with litter and I passed a couple more burnt-out bodies of abandoned motorcars. There were occasional ponds and small watercourses. The damper ground grew broad-leaved scrub, and a somewhat inappropriate grove of eucalyptus trees. Beside the track, heather in several varieties, and then a car in a car park and I was crossing the A4061 on the crest of Mynydd Beili Glas.

A short walk along the verge of the highway, dodging the empty beer and coke cans, polystyrene cups and plastic cartons, the inorganic detritus of passing motorists, and I was ready to scramble down the rough track that would take me to Rhigos. Over my right shoulder was Hirwaun common. Here it was that the red flag flew for the first time, and Hirwaun can claim to be the birthplace of Welsh trades unionism. A battlefield since Norman mercenaries defeated Rhys ap Tewdwr in 1093, through the Merthyr rising of 1831 right down to the bloodless but still bitter coal strike of 1984, Hirwaun is not a place of entirely happy memories for Welsh people. But happy memories for me, for after the 1979 disaster for the Labour party both Tower colliery NUM lodge and the Hirwaun party gave me their nomination to fight the next Parliamentary election in their constituency, although in the end David Morris got the candidacy.

On my left the pool of Craig-y-Llyn. Ahead, the Tower winding gear, since 1994 the last deep mine in South Wales, for though initially it was a drift mine a shaft was sunk in 1946. When closure threatened, rather than accept unemployment, 239 miners pledged £8,000 each of their redundancy money to buy their pit. The day before Christmas eve 1994, the workers, Goitre Tower Anthracite as they called themselves, became the owners of Tower. 'Better than 1947,' as one old collier put it, 'then the government became owners – but it belongs to the miners at last.'

Crossing the main road twice to cut off the double bend I was soon amongst conifers again. The noise of industry and traffic was blanketed by trees, the only sound the sound of the wind whistling gently through the branches of pine. Even here was an upturned colliery tram, the ground mottled with the yellow of iron oxide, and some of the trees were trying to grow on colliery waste. Young larch was intermingled with hazel, and a bank of natural scrub survived on the banks of a pond.

My route was marked with arrows, and the path had obviously been diverted from the original right of way. I soon discovered why, for I became caught up in the maelstrom of a vast opencast coal pit. A twelve-feet-high lap-board fence guarded either side of a busy and very permanent tarmacadam road, specially built to carry the endless procession of trucks going to and from the site. The mining company, Celtic Energy, met their public obligations to the letter, for pedestrians could file through a small overlap in the fence.

A gravelled walkway took me past an artificial pond and new fields established on reseeded slag. Here and there the grass looked better than the natural pasture it replaced, but elsewhere it was yellow and thin. Now for the first time today I walked along hard roads and pavements. The miles pass more easily without mud and puddles, loose earth and stones, tree roots and other vegetation underfoot, as any Roman legionary could tell you.

Rhigos chapel, built in 1880 and refurbished in 1908, was bolted, barred and battered, clearly overtaken by events outside its control. A group of ponies wandered about on grey slag and further down the road paddock railings and a fancy horse-box suggested a more up-market style of horse management. Now I went under a bridge with the Heads of the Valleys dual carriageway above me to find more horseyculture and a vast congregation of caravans resting in their winter quarters.

I turned left on to an old unmaintained road over the hill for Penderyn. The ground was marshy, muddy and poached by herds of horses. It was a desolate countryside, too wet for sheep, too infertile for cattle, ill-drained and poorly fenced. Alder and birch trees grew reasonably well. In case anyone was tempted to drop rubbish there was a large notice:

Dumping Strictly Prohibited.
Clare Co. Co.

I thought I might get lost, but surely not that lost!

The view from the hilltop was more mountainous than industrial. The Church, and a lovely but apparently derelict old vicarage, stands above the more modern houses which are nearer to the main road. Penderyn of course is itself a place of pilgrimage. Dic Penderyn, hanged in Cardiff jail and buried in Aberafan after the Merthyr rising for a killing almost certainly done by someone else, is perhaps himself rather more familiar to most Welsh people than this small and rather straggly village that has given him his name. To the sheep farmers of Wales it is more famous for its annual ram sale, in the heart of Brecknock Hill Cheviot sheep country.

Modern society has an insatiable appetite for stone, for roads, for drainage, for ballast, for concrete and it is so readily available around Penderyn that quarrying is the main industry, but as I turned left to get to the Hepste river I was leaving industrial south Wales behind me. Not that I was entering any garden of Eden, for the ground here is mostly water-logged and infertile.

A succession of stiles, and a confusing over-abundance of signs and arrows, did not make following my path any easier. I skipped around pools and over puddles, the bog grasses already turning green with the promise of spring. A large herd of cattle, gaunt from winter and almost certainly heavily infested with liver fluke, hurriedly munched at a rather inadequate supply of sweet-smelling silage. This farmer keeps big-framed cows, bigger I would say than his fields can really sustain, but I suppose if you want a fair price you need a fair-sized bullock, and there is no point in keeping hardy cattle for which there is no market.

I leaped a style and took a narrow track through a patch of damp scrub, with whips of birch, hazel and stunted oak. On my right hand I could hear the echo of fast-running water. The narrow path became narrower still and tangled with roots and briers. To my right was an almost sheer drop into a swirling river, and I realised that any trip or slip could be my last. The perils of Penrhys had not worried me at all, but above the Hepste river I was very cautious. Although common sense and the universal human experience tells me that I don't have too many useful years left, it suddenly became important to hang on to however many I've got and make the very most of them. Then I joined a proper path, which I should probably have met half a mile sooner. Ash trees grew straight and very tall, reaching up to a distant sky from the deep gorge beneath. I found a flight of wooden steps to help me climb safely down to the bed of the river far below. The roar of the waterfall drowned every other sound, and I was standing at the foot of a wall of tumbling water perhaps fifty feet wide and thirty feet high.

My first thought was of wading through the thigh-deep stream, and then I realised there was an easier and probably drier route. I saw a narrow ledge behind the curtain of the cascade, so I had the new experience of seeing the back view of a giant waterfall. The path was indeed easy to follow, as many had obviously been before me. A few paces downstream and I found a very steep but well-defined path, with cut steps and now and then a strategic handrail. I came breathless to the crest of the further bank and a stern notice:

DANGER.
Deaths have occurred.
Take Care

Now they tell me!

The route to Ystradfellte was well-marked and well-defined. It followed old roads through woods, past planted pines and groves of willow, birch, ash and hazel with an occasional oak on drier ground. There were ruins covered with moss and hidden by trees. When does history start and archaeology end?

I reached a house protected by the security of a succession of locked gates, with stiles for passing pedestrians like myself using the right of way. In a small paddock a glorious quartet of Welsh Cobs, quite the smartest animals I had seen on my pilgrimage so far. After a very pleasant two-mile stroll up the Mellte stream I came to a stone bridge and a tarmacadam road.

On the other side a car park, and at the side a steep drop to the Mellte river. A large party of older schoolchildren, equipped with helmets, torches and rubber boots, trod the path to the water's edge. The river froths and tumbles over dark grey rock, crenellated like a turetted castle wall, before it disappears into the wide, gaping mouth of a great cavern. Fissures opened in the rocks hundreds of thousands of years ago as they cracked under inconceivable pressures. Now bright white lines of pure calcium carbonate, some two centimetres thick, glisten like marble to remind us of the unimaginable power of movements in the earth's crust.

The youngsters followed their leader underground, with a statutory adult at the rear to count them in and count them out. Back in the car park the lettering on the sides of their mini-busses read like a gazetteer

of England; Northampton, Dagenham, Redbridge and Ilford Essex. I wondered, and not for the first time, why children from rural Wales never get a trip to Northampton, Dagenham, Redbridge or even Ilford Essex.

I was tired. I had walked a long way from Penrhys. Not that many miles, but through an infinite diversity of scenery, villages, towns, farms and mines, mountain, forests and rivers and an even greater variety of human experience. At Ystradfellte it was time to call it a day, and I was pleased to see my landrover there to meet me.

THE SECOND DAY

'Poetry, music and dancing stopped. They lost and forgot them all and when times improved in other respects, these things never returned as they had been.' Thus Máire Ní Ghrianna on the Great Famines of Ireland. It would insult the memory of the dead to compare the 2001 outbreak of foot and mouth disease with the Irish Famines, the worst natural disaster to afflict Western Europe since the Black Death. But one thing is certain, since that foot and mouth epidemic nothing in rural Britain will ever be quite as it was before.

It was not just the standstill on all movement of susceptible stock, the virtual house arrests that kept children from school and mothers and fathers from their work, the huge cost of disinfection borne by every sheep and cattle farmer, the agony of seeing animals going unfed and unattended even at lambing time, the impossibility of selling anything to pay the bills or ease the soaring pressure on dwindling fodder supplies, the social isolation with all marts and many country businesses closed down, the sense of being helpless and hopeless, the despair, the desperation, the broken families and the suicides. There was the realisation that farmers and their wives and their sons and daughters and all their relations in related occupations are on their own, marginalised and unimportant. Disposable. The whole culture of a special kind of rural community, self-centred, self-sufficient, inward-looking and complacent, was simply disintegrating about us.

The younger people had no income from the farm. Young men found work in construction, often using their farm-acquired experience with bulldozers and mechanical diggers to cut trenches for pipelines or dig foundations for buildings or roads. Some worked for DEFRA cleansing and disinfecting, or checking the documentation of the few farm-to-farm or farm-to-abattoir movements that were allowed. Others put up fencing to hold stock awaiting slaughter for £4.50 a metre, which compares well with the £1.50 a metre allowed under agri-environmental schemes. Whatever they did, they saw and felt in their pockets the huge differential between earnings from farming and that which could be made from almost any other commercial activity. To quote a popular World War 1 refrain

> How can you keep them down on the farm
> Now that they've seen Paree?

The sheepdog trials, all agricultural shows from the smallest parish bun-fight to the Royal at Llanelwedd itself, the eisteddfodau, private parties and weddings were cancelled or postponed, even funerals went unattended. The biggest youth movement in Wales, the Young Farmers' Club, was effectively closed down for the duration. Once a local committee is suspended who will get it together next year, especially if the younger people have left for greener pastures?

Perhaps 2001 did not make the music and the dancing stop but was just a catalyst for change that was inevitable anyway. We forget that 2000 was also a year of unprecedented misfortune following on two years that were little better. The animal diseases BSE and TB, already so familiar that they were known just by initials, an urban majority unsympathetic to rural values and a currency that made imports cheap and exports nearly impossible had reduced the Welsh livestock industry, which is effectively the whole of Welsh farming, to a sorry state before F and M. When times improve in other respects things will never return to what they had been.

As I walked from Ystradfellte to cross the south-west corner of the Great Forest of Brecknock and over the Black Mountains to Llanddeusant I was confronted by a succession of rough and ready rustic bill-boards saying 'Foot and Mouth. Keep Out.' Some farmers at least, despite all paths being officially open, were using foot and mouth as a fine excuse to keep them permanently shut. I was not deterred.

I was now off the coal and on the limestone. It was everywhere, great lumps of it sticking up out of the green turf, rock clumps and crags of it all around me as I walked along. Here was a giant kiln that once turned stone into quicklime and the giant pedestal of the old loading bay. A broken rail still lay half buried in the ground, a sad remnant from what had once been a busy industrious scene.

Now the traveller's *vade-mecum*, my Ordnance Survey 1:50,000 map, let me down, or rather I failed to follow it with sufficient care. I have always prided myself on my map-reading expertise, and love these magic maps with their delightful symbols and incredible detail. In years past I travelled hundreds of miles through the forests of Guyana and the wilds of north-west Canada without any comparable guide, but more recent experience in Wales and Ireland has made me lazy, and I rely on maps to get me wherever I want to go. As I wasted valuable minutes of a deteriorating March day trying to find exactly where I was, I wondered at the courage of earlier pilgrims who climbed these jagged hills, up and down these deep-cut valleys, without plan or precedent. The surprise is not that they found their journey hard going but that they ever arrived in St Davids at all. Presumably the sun and the stars, with maybe a little help from the standing stones, were sufficient signposts for them.

Soon enough I found a bearing on Blaen-Nedd Isaf farmhouse. I scrambled down the bank to find an unlikely mixture of goings-on in the context of modern agriculture. For a start there was every kind of poultry from geese through gamecocks to guinea fowl scratching around. Then there were the cattle. Tiny prong-horned Welsh Blacks and Galloway crosses. These last were probably related to the herd on the nearby Cnewr estate which the McTurk family brought down from Scotland over thirty years ago. You might think that their journey was not really necessary, as Wales has its own breed of tough, black hill cattle, and if you really want to breed the horns off you can do that too.

The Scottish sheep, on the other hand, and here I'm referring to the Cheviot and not the Blackfaced breed although there are a few of these about as well, have proved real money spinners and have made a lasting mark on the Breconshire landscape. In the early nineteenth century a flood of Scottish sheep men moved into upland Wales. They brought sheepdog trialling to Bala and their sheep to Breconshire. They built huge farms at Belfont, Forest Lodge, Cnewr and Plas-y-Gors. All except Plas-y-Gors have survived, and that is the huge ruin that you can still see just off the Senni to Ystradfellte road.

The difficulty of maintaining up to forty miles of stone walls to enclose the new estates proved too much for some of these enterprising Scotsmen and farms became tenanted. In 1853 Mr Rogerson, a tenant of fat-cat John Claypole at Cnewr, is believed to have walked his flock much of the way from Scotland. The Cheviot sheep, with their fine wool and meaty bodies, were not only a success on the Brecon Beacons. The Knight family in Devon walked a flock all the way from Scotland to Exmoor. A few years ago Asa Pinney, currently secretary of the South Wales Sheepdog Trialling Association, repeated their journey, like some latter-day Thor Heyerdahl crossing the Pacific on the Kon Tikki he proved it could be done.

I was directed cheerfully enough by a busy farming man, who was obviously as accustomed to stray people as I am to stray sheep, to the footbridge over the Neath river. I negotiated my way through a cattle yard crowded with some of the smallest black cows and heifers, not forgetting the tiny bull, I have ever seen. At £1,200 each what a fortune would have gone into somebody's pocket if these had caught foot and mouth! It is every hill farmers' dilemma, keep hardy animals that suit the environment and produce very little, or bigger animals that aren't really suited to mountain life.

It was a steep climb from the river but a fairly short one. Now I was on the heathery top with four or five miles to go before the head-waters of the Tawe. This was easy walking, and well signposted by a visitor friendly if paternal National Park. You could see by the hoof-prints that the cattle had been running out well into the winter, and sheep were still grazing in March. Heather is far less nutritious than young grass, but it does provide something right through the year. The sorry ruin of a farmstead and a substantial sheep-fold confirmed that I was on the right track, a track that had once been a highway, for there were the remnants of dykes on either side.

As my path skirted the limestone outcrop of Carreg Cadno I saw the ridge of Bannau Brycheiniog etched with snow, a lingering drift of it nearly two miles long. There were countless sink holes along the way, where the acid run-off from the overlying peat had eaten into the rock. Some were small and insignificant, but others were serious craters and this was no place for walking on a dark night or misty day. The thin March sunshine was warm enough for larks to rise and sing, and specks of marble flashed like white jewels in the bare rock. The tourist brochures for the Brecon Beacons are full of pictures of pretty villages in the Usk valley and the greener grass of the red sandstone country, but there is far greater peace and tranquillity between the mountain tops and the mining valleys than ever there is at Llangorse or Crickhowell or on Mynydd Illtyd.

Then suddenly peace was destroyed and tranquillity gone as a pair of low-flying military jets skimmed the ground on some sinister and expensive exercise. There are far worse places to scratch a living from the land – Afghanistan or Iraq for instance.

Just before the long and steep descent into the Upper Swansea valley I had to climb a style which took me into a fenced enclosure with an explanatory notice:

> We are Studying the Effects of Not Grazing
> the Vegetation in this Plot.

The effects were very marginal, similar vegetation to that in the grazed area but rather more of it. An occasional thorn and an ash tree had made it to four feet high. So much for the notion that without sheep the mountains would be an impenetrable jungle of scrub! There were big-sink holes or pot-holes, up to eight feet across, some made safe with railway sleepers, and one big cave was sealed with a concrete panel.

Now houses again, and I go down a steep pitch to Penwyllt. Industry is not dead in the Upper Swansea Valley, for jagged pinnacles of limestone tower above the pit of a still very much working quarry. The railway lines that once took the stone down to Swansea were lifted forty years ago. The terrace of quarrymens' cottages have been taken over by the South Wales Caving Club. The pastures were grazed very tight by ewes brought down for lambing, and an abandoned baling machine shows that these fields are considered sufficiently flat and fertile to grow mowable crops of hay. I walked down a street of houses and crossed the A4067 road by the Gwyn Arms.

The Upper Swansea Valley is a land of hard farming, mines, hard men and quarries, but it has a magic of its own. The extraordinary Craig-y-nos where singer Adelina Patti built her castle near the sky was itself a big employer in her day, and still is now that it has become a country park and visitor attraction. The great caves of Dan yr Ogof, until recently desecrated by a herd of fibreglass dinosaurs grazing by the roadside, retain most of their majesty and power despite the pervasive spirit of Walt Disney and the best efforts of the Wales Tourist Board with their notorious enthusiasm for tacky commercialisation.

As I took the path up Cwm Haffes I met the ultimate absurdity, a muddy field enclosing a troupe of bad tempered South American alpaca and one fat Dartmoor sheep. On the other side was a large collection of miscellaneous horses and a couple of donkeys. The ground beneath their feet had been trodden into a treacle. They all wore unnecessary waterproof rugs and would have been far better off on drier ground, with or without their mackintoshes. Donkeys in particular hate having their feet wet all the time. I was told that the tourists love saying hello to the animals.

The changeable March weather changed for the worse, wet and cold, and despite a rising wind the visibility was poor. This is a land of rocky crags, limestone pavements, sink holes and peat lagoons. The rock had eroded, weathered and split to leave deep cracks and giant boulders.. I had to proceed with care, for I have broken both legs in recent years and have been given a very clear warning of the likely consequences of another careless step or foolish leap. It was not a pleasant afternoon to lie immobilised on some lonely ledge with little prospect of being found before the Spring Bank Holiday.

In a grassy hollow I stumbled across the sink of the Giedd river. Here the water flows into the mountainside to disappear as completely and abruptly as the children of Hamelin. Unlike that legendary lost

generation it does however reappear some half a mile away and eventually join the Tawe upstream of Ystradgynlais.

I trudged north and was soon floundering through the marshy ground skirting the banks of the Twrch river. At last I was on familiar ground and thank goodness, for the day was passing and I was enveloped by wet and windy clouds scudding through the gap of Twrch Fechan. My own sheep seldom walk this far from home, but I have ridden up here scores of times on one horse or another. I have picnicked by this river, caught its wild brown trout and collected pretty coloured stones from the river bed. I know my way by the tilt of the horizon, a familiar hollow or the outline of a friendly rock.

Now I jump the stream below Coffer Sali Morris, where the unfortunate Sali Morris hid her egg and butter money on her weekly trip home from Ystradgynlais, only to have it all buried under a landslip on just such a wild evening as this. I could have seen, if I could see in the foul weather, the great Cairn of Carreg Las. What long forgotten people piled up that enormous heap of stones, and why?

All I can see is the rain, and just about make out through the mist the next fifty yards of my pilgrimage. Below Cairn y Gigfran, home of ravens, I am blown flat on my back and pick myself up only to fall down again. Then my foothold improves, and beneath the clouds I can see the green fields of Carmarthenshire. Beyond the Towy valley, the land of milk and money, lie the Cambrian mountains and the heartland of Welsh Wales.

As I stumble frozen and soaked through the Gelligron mountain gate I pass the James' Cheviot sheep just starting to settle for the night in the shelter of the hazel and alder roots. All are heavy in lamb, and each is almost a mirror image of every other. You surely don't have to be a sheep farmer to appreciate the effort, enthusiasm, expertise and experience that has gone into breeding such a flock.

This corner of east Carmarthenshire must contain as high a density of top class stock farming talent as anywhere else on earth. Here our lives revolve around the cattle sales and sheep sales, the weekly mart and the farmers' co-op, shearing and hay harvest, gathering the mountain flocks, lambing, ear-marking and shearing again. The names of these farms and farmers are as familiar to those of us in the trade as any superstars of sport or show business, but beyond that closed circle they are nobody.

In Llanddeusant you are a sheep farmer or nothing, and when I was first elected to the local council every member except one, the schoolmaster, was farming. We know one another not by name but by farm, as Willie Pencarreg, Glyn Penrhiw, Arwel Nantyrodyn or Val Gorsddu. There are a handful in other occupations, the retired and a few holiday homes, but they are marginal to the mainstream of community life. The changing fortunes of the farming families as they evolve between generations are the substance of our local history.

Now I have reached the last mile. My tough working clothes have lost their resilience in the face of the storm. The battle to stay dry is lost, but the high hedge banks of Cwmsawdde protect me from the gale and though wet I am no longer cold.

On top of the final hill stands the Youth Hostel. Even now it is threatened with closure, but the building itself is a store of memories. Before its present role it was a public house, the Red Lion. In the 1960s the middle-aged daughters of the last publican used to come from Cardiff to my farm, not a mile and a half along the road towards the mountain, for a caravanning weekend each summer. They told me how their late father grew so rich off the Irishmen working on Llyn y Fan dam during the first World War that he retired to considerable ease and comparative affluence.

But this oblong box of Sawdde stone has a longer history. It was once a row of miners' cottages. Until the second half of the eighteenth century Llanddeusant was a parish of industry, mining and commerce. There were at least three blacksmiths' shops, a woollen mill, a dying factory, corn mills, lime kilns, quarries and a lead mine, and on the boundary of the parish a small iron foundry. There was once over ten times the present population in what since became the most sparsely populated parish in Wales, so no wonder you can't walk far without stumbling over the fallen stones of some long abandoned dwelling! The cottages still called Turkey and Spain were the homes of expatriate miners who brought their skills from over the sea. Llanddeusant was a centre for immigration, as the Rhondda valleys became in the following century. When the settlements of Llwynypia and Tonypandy were no more than a huddle of pig cotes and cattle sheds the mill wheels of Llanddeusant were turning and our men were going down the mines.

At my journey's end, the Church. The present building is little more than seven hundred years old, but as it was rebuilt on a previous foundation dated between AD370 and AD570 it can fairly claim to be one of the oldest Christian religious houses in the country. I have followed in the footsteps of St Paulinus, for he too walked this way from Penrhys. Here, the twin brothers Potolius and Notolius established a monastic settlement, although no trace can be seen today of the fabric of their cells and their little oratory.

My pilgrimage is over. It is the magic of Wales that there is such variety, so many ways to use the resources of the earth to make life bearable and productive and such an infinite mulitiplicity of human experience in so small a space. Yet I am no nearer to solving the impenetrable mystery which baffles every pilgrim, to which no advance in science and technology or political organisation gives any signpost along the way, the ultimate riddle of the meaning and purpose of life. The question without answer. The journey without end.

THEIR LAND
THEY SHALL LOSE

Jon Gower

THEIR LAND THEY SHALL LOSE

It was a God-given day, snow softening the craggy outlines of the Carmarthen Vans, the ridge-backed range of what people in south Wales like to call mountains and which Tibetan north Walians, from Llanrwst to Llandegai would dismiss as hills. A yaffle, a green woodpecker gave raucous and maniacal greeting as I entered the graveyard of Llanddeusant church. Llan-ddeu-sant. The church of two saints? A kindly vicar had posted a note which served to explain things. Despite the fact that this small church in the shadow of the mountains is dedicated to St. Simon and St. Jude there is a belief that the name comes from two brothers, the euphoniously named Potolius and Notolius who came here with St. Paulinus from a religious community in Llantwit Major in the Vale of Glamorgan. This is how one documentarian of his day, Wrmonoc, a Breton monk put it:

> Having received his master's blessing and kiss of peace, and leave to depart, he went forth and sought the seclusion of a certain desert place which adjoined his father's possessions. There he built a cell and a little oratory.

The poet Harri Webb got it right when he entitled one of his volumes *The Green Desert*. In this green desert platoons of sheep, the right side of the county line – Carmarthenshire, not Breconshire – escaped the ravages of foot and mouth. Not far away, at Storey Arms, the roadside tents, the temporary sheep enclosures of the crisis are a recent memory now, but not so recent that the pain of the killing fields is dissipated.

The church as it now stands was built in the 14th century under the patronage of Lady Anne. Local legend has it – and this area is a wellspring of legend, with Llyn y Fan and its underwater maiden only a crow's hop away – that the church was first erected in the tiny hamlet of Twynllanan, a couple of miles away but that under cover of darkness the stones mysteriously decamped to the present site. I'm put in mind of what a French writer once said – 'Myth is very old gossip.'

Many of the graves are mossy now but as is true for so many churchyards it is the infant mortality that most vividly conjurs up the past. 'William Griffiths 3 years July 11 1856.'

I try the door but it is locked like so many countryside churches. Signs proclaim you are being watched all over the Welsh countryside. That's because people will nick just about anything. A theft occurred in Powys some years back which proves this categorically. A Powys county council truck was stolen and this despite the fact that it was in full local authority livery and was hooked up to a snowplough. Yes, it disappeared, in broad daylight, with no reported sightings. Allowing for the rare possibility of alien abduction, maybe to a cold planet such as Pluto, where a snowplough might come in handy, this remains an unsolved case.

If you wander from church to church you can become a sort of amateur epidemiologist, tracing illness and it spread. There were big flu epidemics and some churches have built memorials, like those to the slain in what idiots called the Great War. I wonder what the old herbalists, the Physicians of Muddfai, who ran a sort of university of alternative medicine in a village only a few miles away, would have prescribed when the epidemics of flu swept these parts. They had a cure for most things. If you had gangrene all you had to do was take 'a black toad which is only able to crawl and beat it with a stick until it becomes furious and so that it swells until it dies, and take it and put it into an earthenware cooking pot and close the lid on it so that the smoke may not escape nor the air get into it, and burn it in the pot until it is ashes and apply the ashes to the gangrene.' That simple. And dealing with quinzy was just a matter of letting blood from beneath your two arms and from the vein of the head and putting a little plaster of mallow, linseed and a little butter without salt around your neck and at the base of the tongue.

I head west, noting how glaciation has smoothed the tops of the hills like a plasterer's trowel, indented in places with small ornamental nicks. This was an ice river flowing.

The hedgerows are alive with vernal birdsong. It may be that the blackbird and the chaffinch are our commonest birds but in this stretch of countryside it seems that robins rule, with a territorial male singing

its tiny lungs out every few hundred yards. This is the time when
territory-claiming changes the robin's personality. In winter, armed
with a wriggling mass of meal-worms, a gardener might be able to get
two birds to feed side by side on his hands. But as the nesting season
opens they become arch-rivals, willing to fight to death for an acre of
garden.

The quality of light here reminds me of other high places, like the
lunar sweep of the Altiplano in Bolivia, or the High Atlas as you
negotiate the Tizi 'n' Test, a road for drivers with deathwishes to enjoy.
The hills here in Wales, and the limpid sky give me a sense of
exhilaration, of epiphany almost. William Williams, Pantycelyn, the
industrious hymn writer, would have felt the same sort of thing in the
late eighteenth century when he saw the aurora borealis, the Northern
Lights turning the Carmarthenshire sky kaleidoscope.

'I was called out of my house with great urgency and alarm; the
whole sky was red, pale blue, yellow, purple, ruddy; the colour of
blood, of the dawn, of porphyry, of amber; all the colours of the
rainbow, and like to it with the exception that the whole sky was
dancing and playfully interweaving, as if to provoke shock and fear in
the guilty part of the world, but indescribable joy in the inheritors of
eternal life.'

Now I am not what you might call a conventionally religious man
and epiphanies by their nature are not dime-a-penny experiences but
they do come every once in a while, supercharged moments when the
senses are hyper-alert, and the world, is, well, more *lit* than at any other
time.

One Halcyon summer, working on Bardsey island I was swimming
in Y Cafn when a school of Risso's dolphins starburst out of the water
having sighted a killer whale sharking through the waters of the sound.
My heart surged with that spectacle. Recently, at Point Reyes on the
California coast I took in the great sweep of sand that reaches out to a
finger like promontory of rock and felt an impossible joy well up
within and started shuddering with laughter. It may have been a
welling up of relief after watching a spectacularly short marriage
crumble, but there was something about that sea and landscape that
reminded me of my favourite patch of this planet, the silky sands of

Cefn Sidan on the Llanelli coast, which also has a sweep of bay, and stretches of dunes and slacks, rimmed by pine forest, a mirror image of the Californian scene. But, being America, the landscape I beheld was bigger and had a titanic impact. Here, in Carmarthenshire, my county, standing on a tarmac by-way, looking at the cotton blossom snow on the brackeny spines of rock, with the sky boundless, as the late R. S. put it, I had a comparable surge of joy. It may be a hoary old chestnut of a cliché but I was glad to be alive.

Now that I am on the verge of finding myself in my anecdotage this might be a good place to pause for my favourite R.S. story. I was spending the night in the great poet's home near Aberdaron and this at a time when I didn't know he was a poet and we were discussing Wordsworth, my precocious schoolboy arrogance informing every trifling fact I offered as a gew-gaw before him. 'Wordsworth was a pantheist poet,' I proudly informed him. 'Do you know what that means?' Yes, that's what I asked the greatest pantheist poet of the twentieth century. Akin to asking 'Mr. Eliot, did you know that an anagram of your name is toilets?'

The village of Gwynfe has two kinds of kites, the ones that spiral around a sculpture outside the community hall and the real one that twists on the wind above the place. It is a symbol of conservation success. A hundred years ago this beautiful bird of prey was clinging by a talon to existence in Wales having been trapped and shot everywhere else. Guarded by farmers, locals and the Kite Committee (which included Colonel H. Morrey Salmon, R.S. Thomas and a great naturalist – William Condry) the bird was spared the attentions of egg collectors and now a healthy population swallowtails across Welsh skies. Beautiful it is – with its silver streaked head and lemon eyes and russet plumage – but stupid too. Shakespeare warned that when the kite nests you should 'look to lesser linen' referring to the kite's habit of raiding clothes' lines for nesting material. But what it takes to the nest can, on occasion confuse the bird. One bird in Wales spent a whole nesting season trying to incubate a yellow tennis ball!

The neat, linear village of Gwynfe is notable for having a chapel in the church grounds. The churchwarden, George Fleming, who farms some fifty acres nearby , explained that as 'the church grew in strength

in the 1500s and 1600s, the mother church decided to donate the chapel to Gwynfe. In 1899 they built a new church and the little chapel became defunct – they even lost the key . . .'

I begin the climb up towards Trichrug past Blaen-Llynnant farm. The map's contracting contour lines and imagined panoramas promises quite a view for at the top the whole of Tywi valley opens out. The Tywi is one of those rivers that shape Carmarthenshire, tumbling from Llyn Brianne where its headwaters are now gathered behind a dam, then torrentially snaking through the tropical green gulches of Rhandirmwyn. These oak woodlands come alive in summer. Male pied flycatchers, our most dapper summer bird visitors with their black and white plumage, look as if they are wearing tuxedos. Shy redstarts – *steort* meant tail in Old English – hide away their beauty, but a glimpse of a male bird, with its fiery chestnut tail, white forehead, black throat and grey mantle makes all the patient skulking it takes to sight one very worthwhile. And then completing a trio of birds which travel all the way fom Africa to summer in these woods is the wood warbler, a yellow-breasted denizen of glade and overhang, whose song is a single note which speeds up to a whistling trill.

Downstream from where I stand is one of my favourite winter haunts, the flood-meadows of Dryslwyn, where in winter the ox-bows and flashes swell and thousands of wildfowl converge – mergansers and goosanders, whistling wigeons, pochards and little grebes. There used to be a flock of white fronted geese that honked and trumpeted here too, but year by year their numbers dwindled until one winter there was just one bird and the next there were none. It may be that as the climate has changed they have taken to wintering in the west, investigating the peats of Ireland. But I still miss the sound of them in night skies, sounding the honking clarion calls of migration and linking Carmarthenshire with that huge mass of land in the far north, with the west coast of Greenland, with Uummannaq and Savissivik and with the Mackenzie basin of Canada. If I craned the mind's eye a little higher I can see past Dryslwyn to where the the river widens as it makes stately and fish-sustaining process down past the county town of Carmarthen towards the estuary of the three rivers, where it joins the Taf and Gwendraeth to make a half starfish, marking the edge of land.

My lungs ar working like bellows now as I climb the steep track upwards – and I'm thinking too much city life, not enough country air! As I crest the ridge with a tumble of ravens flighting over the crag to my left and a forestry plantation to my right I spy below me Garn Goch, the red hill. This is an imposing iron age hill fort if ever there was. One could be mistaken for thinking that red is a reference to the brackeny brown aspect of it on a winter's day like this. This is a land of hill forts. In the west and south west of Carmarthenshire over seventy hill forts and enclosures have been found, while there are some six hundred in Wales as a whole. Some of them are very big, covering over twenty acres. Sir J.E. Lloyd in 'A History of Carmarthenshire' explains that Garn Goch is actually made up of one large camp, 'Y Gaer Fawr' and a smaller satellite fort known as 'the Lower Camp' with a third fort above Coed Llwyn Maendy. Although this site is overlooked by higher ground it is surrounded by two streams and in days of primitive weapons would have been well-nigh impregnable.

I look up at the craggy outline of Trichrug and make a mental note to retun to these hills in May when trips of dotterel, wading birds that nest in high places, such as Scotland's Cairngorms stop by on their way north to forage for insects among the stones, dining on spiders and crowberries. Some of these Carmarthenshire hills are traditional resting sites for the birds during their long passage, although I have never seen one. But I find solace in what R.S. Thomas, with whom I spent many a fine day birdwatching, said: 'Ah but a rare bird is only rare when you're not there.'

A history lecture given on the site, in the days when interested parties would travel by carriage as far as Dyffryn Ceidrich mill, by one Edward Laws of Tenby posited that the iron age hill forts weren't dwelling places but rather 'refuges for a sparse population who lived in the valleys below, and that when danger appeared the braves of the tribe hurried their women, children, long-faced oxen, hairy little sheep, and great long-legged pigs into these little camps, where they made a stand until relieved by their neighbours.' But not at Garn Goch where 'they had an excellent water supply, gigantic works, which proved the co-operation of a very considerable population, and engineering of a very different order from the little cliff castles. The inhabitants probably lived with their flocks and herds within the walls.'

It is an imposing site and a sense of its impregability came as I followed a green lane down towards Dyffryn Ceidrich. Not having received the necessary hours of commando training, negotiating the mud was enough to turn me into a seventeen stone contortionist, sometimes straddling the two banked sides, or crashing through a copse of trees in a patch so damp that not only the branches I looked to for support but the trees themselves snapped off as I tried to cling to something, anything. The First World War gave us terms such as trenchcoat and trenchfoot, as humanity was mired in the mud of the Somme. I had a brief glimpse of how fighting in mud is fighting against mud.

I was relieved to reach the valley bottom and head for Llangadog. Crossing Carreg Sawdde Common I realised that serendipity had smiled upon me and I would arrive in time to see the Wales versus Italy rugby match. I watched Wales pour on the points as the inn-keeper poured me a good few pints of Bass. After hearing that France had taken the wind out of England's imperious sails I decided make a night of it to stay for the Scotland–Ireland game.

Morning saw me indulging in a spot of impromptu birdwatching. My tally by the time the toast arrived was more than impressive. There was a woodcock, its plumage like shadow-dappled bracken fronds, a plump-bellied partridge, a buzzard and a lone red kite. The birds were stuffed specimens admittedly but it still look some skill to identify the owls – barn, tawny, and long-eared, and an arrestingly wide winged snowy owl with piercing lemon eyes, a jay, a gannet, a cormorant and a pair of cuckoos that stared sullenly and glass-eye-ily from the cases. Silas Wegg, the con-artist with the wooden leg in Dickens' 'Our Mutual Friend' would have enjoyed ferreting around in the dining room at the Castle. Another quick inventory: a stuffed otter, raised up on its hindlegs sported a black woollen glove on one paw, a copy of 'Y Bibl Cysegr Lan' which once belonged to the Parchedig or Reverend Peter Williams, not one but five jester's hats, some parachuting clowns – one with a floppy hat and yellow waistcoat parachuting down from the original oak beams, the complete works of Byron, a pretty authoritative set of reference books suitable for setting and adjudicating pub quizzes, a native American amulet with decorative feathers, a porcelain Chinese dragon flying east, a grim collection of pole traps, a brass statuette of a British bobby on the beat, an old safe, a miniature coracle, a brass moon and stars, a fencing sword, a collection of miniature whiskies, a book about the Battle of the Somme and a framed certificate which announced that J.O. Griffiths of the Royal Fusiliers was disabled and honorably discharged from the Great War in 1914.

After one of the best breakfasts I've had in Wales – rivalled only by the Grapes in Maentwrog – I asked mein hosts about the provenance of all this stuff? The pub dates back to 1756 and in the old days it owned all the land down to the river.

It would have been a place to slake serious thirst, with river water for the animals and something stronger for the men who had marched with them. The drovers – 'pre Texan, pre gaucho, pre-Aussie overlander' should have had big films made about them, much as the Westerns conjured up the cowboy life. One gets the feeling that Wales is too small, the horizon too close up, and the skies above not big enough. It's not a road movie, or 'The Big Country' sort of topography.

Leaving Llangadog, the skies had that rain-laden heaviness you encounter in the Dutch paintings of Albert Cuyp. The local cement products factory proclaimed proudly and sensibly that it had been 129 days since the last reportable accident which was an improvement on the previous best of 243. I paused as I crossed over the river bridge to watch a pair of mute swans drift by. Collective nouns for birds sometimes capture an essential of theirs, a charm of nightingales, an exhultation of larks, a spring of teal, a parliament of rooks and a murder of ravens. I think that the collective noun for swans should be a serenity. A serenity of swans. Yes, that should do it. To look at, at least.

The mute swan is the largest bird in Britain with wings strong enough to break a man's arm should he be foolhardly enough to get too close to the nest. There is a legend that Richard the Lionheart first brought swans home from Cyprus after the Third Crusade but they were probably in Britain long before that. They used to be captive birds and were only released into the wild a little over a century ago, since

when they have become an essential component of the waterside scene. Mute they are not, as a anyone who has head them hissing and snorting would readily testify.

A curlew flies overhead, uttering a plaintive 'coor-li' which puts me in mind of W.B. Yeats and Phillip Warlock, two artists who found inpsiration in this bird's call and song.

I look back at the brackeny ridge of Garn Goch, find a small path on the map that will take me to Llansadwrn and walk off under dishwatery skies. Wild strawberries are in flower and I think of how the fruit will be a delight to foraging field mice when they chance upon them in the summer. There's a lot of mud to negotiate and I make awkward progress like a man with rubber legs attempting to dance the rhumba.

The historian John Davies once opined that the two finest British inventions are bitter beer and the Ordnance Survey map. Sustained by the idea of slaking my thirst later on with one fine invention I stop awhile to peruse another. The one and quarter inch to the mile Landranger 146, for Lampeter, Llandovery and the surrounding area contains a poetic litany of place names: Llettyrcadwgan, Coed Caer Bedw, Bron-y-glyn, Ynys Rhyd, Pentir Bach, Glasallt Fawr, Gelli Felen, Llwynywormwood, Rhyblid. And there are questions too: Did the well at Ffynnon Ddeiliog – leafy well – fill with leaves or was it in a leafy bower? Were the magpies at Llwynpiod – the magpies' grove – particularly raucous to lend their names to the place?

Llansadwrn is still asleep, with only two young girls abroad at this hour. They each sell me an enchanting smile before giggling away. I take the back road towards Talley, accompanied for much of the way by buzzards – as many as nine in the air at the same time. Their numbers are now much recovered since the unnatural plague of myxamatosis took away their main food and the population plummeted.

A lone jogger lopes by, the only other person on foot I have seen during this stretch. When George Borrow walked around Wales he was forever bumping into people on the roads – tinkers, travellers, farmhands – but nowadays a man on foot is a notifiable incident. I pass another hill-fort but calculate that too much of my day will go in climbing it, so press on.

Descending into Talley, looking back at the hamlet of Halfway, there is a hillside stippled with young tree plantings, the ridges pixillated by pines, like the olive-studded landscapes of Greece or Spain. Stands of birch, with their tell-tale purple hue seem to smoke with place colour.

That prominent peregrine, Giraldus Cambrensis, whose accounts of Wales in the twelfth century tell us so much – about beavers in the rivers, about the nature of our choral singing (in their musical concerts they do not sing in unison like the inhabitants of other countries, but in many parts) and how we kept our teeth white by chewing willow wands – knew Talley. He knew 'a poor house, in a rough and sterile spot, surrounded by woods on every side and beyond measure innaccessible.' The place had a Celtic church before the Romans but the ruins that now stand as the central landmark belonged to the Premonstraterian order who had established many communities in England and Scotland but Talley was their only Welsh outpost. It was probably established by Prince Rhys ap Gruffydd who also founded the Cistercian abbey at Strata Florida and was a big benefactor of Whitland. Talley was a much poorer cousin of both as the account ledgers show. In 1291 Talley's income was £8 16s and 6d per year while Strata Florida's was £2,600.

Like the Cistercians the Premonstraterians loved solitary places and agriculture. Their motto was 'devotion and service' and there was a period, in the thirteenth century, when the Abbott of Talley was also Bishop of St David and apart from the bishop the place would have an average of 8 canons who administered sacraments in adjoining churches. By 1433 the Abbey's possesssions were wasted by misrule and there was a further body blow with Henry VIII's Dissolution of the Monasteries Act which meant that Talley was no longer an abbey after 1537.

The finest medieval Welsh poet, and one of our finest poets of any century, Dafydd ap Gwilym spent his last years here. I stood at the edge of one of Talley's lakes willing a seagull to appear so that I could fit the image of the bird to the remembered lines of Dafydd's poem '*Yr Wylan*', The Seagull, shivery lines full of glints of sunlight, in which he compares the bird to a nun, unsullied and pure. He also wrote about Talley where 'The monks fixed on a beautiful spot/To watch and weep – for all, to feel and pray, Allure to brighter worlds, and lead the way.'

The monks here were laymen and didn't preach, confess or exercise any spiritual functions, they wore white cassocks, caps and cloaks and were known as the white monks, or canons.

Tomos Lewis the blacksmith is also buried here, the author of the Welsh hymn '*Wrth gofio'i riddfannau'n yr ardd*'. As you'd expect from a man who worked hard with his hands the theology at work in this popular song is as tough as nails as the hymnwriter recalls Christ's agony in the garden, his sweat like beads of blood, and the scoring of the whip on his back.

In the house next door to the Abbey lives Eric Jones , M.B.E, (for services to forestry) and his wife Gwyneth. He is a keen quoits player, a walker of the hills and a gardener – 'I raise enough potatoes for the two of us in a year – there's a good soil in Talley I can tell you.' His family was one of those fifty families forced to leave the Eppynt during the war years and 'every one of them a Welsh-speaker.' In Cilcennyn village the school shut, 'everything shut in the village.' Families broke their hearts and were only given four weeks notice to leave and his father took the family to live in Gwernogle near Brechfa.' It's an episode captured in a powerful piece by Iorwerth Peate, called 'Their Land they shall Lose,' recently translated by Meic Stephens. At Waun Lwyd farm Peate finds a lorry at the back of the house and at the front he finds an old woman of eighty-two.

'I shall never forget the scene: she had set an old chair at the far end of the yard and was sitting there like a graven image, staring intently at the upland with tears streaming down her cheeks. She had been born there, and her father and grandfather before her. She was leaving today and now she was spending her last few moments to take it all in, with one rich gaze at the ancient mountain, or perhaps recalling all the days of her life in the old smallholding. I don't know which; but there she was, and I could only see her grief and foreboding. I felt as if I has stumbled upon a sacrament and I tried to get away quietly.'

Eric Jones goes back to Eppynt once a year 'to the old home because I believe my heart belongs to the rock.' His father took the uprooting badly, because he came 'from generations of shepherds and he died when he was thirty six and I think he broke his heart.' Eric's voice falters as he redacts the story.

Reading a slim history of Talley by Fred S. Price I chanced upon an account of one of the parish's less heralded sons – 'Arthur Lovel' otherwise known as David Coethyn Williams, who was educated at the nearby Llansawel Academy and Llandovery College, rejected a classical scholarship to Oxford and headed for Glasgow. He published prolifically and his titles include 'Meditation' 'The Ideal Man' 'Concentration' 'Beauty of Tone, 'Volo, or the Will, 'How to Think' while his 'Ars Vivendi, or the Art of Living' went though seven editions and he became the leader of something called the Ars Vivendi league.

Standing the church side of the lake I recalled that a good friend of mine, the poet Bryn Griffiths, once penned some lines on this very spot, in a poem which starts

> Here above the scattered stones of Talley Abbey, a bird bullets
> Down the sky, drops down to die and stuns the clear air,
> To where the lake lies dreaming in the still winter's day.

> The eye, caught in the dark valley's timeless clutch,
> Sees the twin worlds of air and water work once more –
> A finned and diving bird below the water's floor.

The poem ends with another bird which

> . . . Spins in the trawled sky over Talley; and only a dog's distant bark
> Disturbs the valley's silence and the slow dusk of Mabinogion dark.

Arthur Morgan, lives in Porth Selyf, a house facing the abbey, and named after the western gate. It was built in 1780 or before. He thinks the place has real spiritual connections:

'That's St Michael's and all Angels out there – there used to be a church of the same name up the hill and the graveyard's still there. There's a church of St Michel in France, and a St Michael's Mount in Cornwall. There's a ley-line that connects them. A man called round here once wanting to know where St Michaels's church was. I showed him the church but he said that's not the one, it's not old enough . . .' The other one was.

The road climbs up to give a good vantage point over Talley's two lakes where small flotillas of tufted ducks bob. I then arrive at Moelfre, a pretty ordinary house surrounded by an extraodinary statuary. The garden is full of heads that resemble those on Easter Island and fecund females, gravid and wooden, squat around the base of the garden shed. A man appears, and introduces himself as the musician and sculptor Francis Dempsey, who carves all of these arresting works. When I tell him about the reason behind my walk he tells me a story about the German film director Werner Herzog, who walked right across Germany to see a dying woman.

I asked Francis, a London Irishman about the work in the garden. He has set a steering wheel atop some lengths of guttering from which hang assorted pieces of metal. He explains that this is a sculpture you can play as a musical instrument and that as the mood takes him he might stand there in the front garden summoning up a tune from the Heath Robinson affair. He imagines the sound as being similar to the bell of Talley abbey which would have been carried on the wind to this spot. The bell itself, a giant affair, was taken to Exeter cathedral where it still chimes.

Francis used to play the flute and the soprano saxophone but he lost a few of his teeth which put pay to that. He sometimes serenades the streams nearby 'because when the water finds certain places in the burn it can set up a really good rhythm – thrump, thrump.' His most ambitious scheme to employ Nature as accompanist involved a piano which he tried to raise into the branches of a tree, creating the Aeolian harp to end all Aeolian harps. The enterprise was doomed by the sheer weight of the instrument and when Francis tried to prise off the cast iron base it fractured and so did the plan.

Nowadays he is learning the cello and aims to master some of Bach's more testing pieces. I left him standing in the wonderment of carvings.

The road leading away from the house is a proud avenue of ancient oaks which might have been seeded by the monks, or at least in my imagination.

You cross the Cothi at Edwinford mansion, Rhydodyn, which had just been put on the market. In its recent history goings on at the place raised a good few local eyebrows when the owner bequeathed the place to the butler.

Richard Fenton who penned 'Tours in Wales' passed this way once, noting 'an old Mansion, pretty large, lying low on the banks of the Cothy, which winds under the beautiful wooded Hills near it. There is a large walled Garden, a greater part of which is mud, said to be the best for fruit. To characterize the different farm Offices, there occur several well executed figures in lead painted, such as a large Pig near the Piggery, Hay makers near the Haggard, and at the Stables or Kennel an admirable fowler. Near the house are shewn 13 large Trees planted the year Thos Williams Esq., of this house was Sheriff, by him and his 12 Javelin Men after their return from the Spring Assizes – a central tree with 12 others round it.'

When the Rhydodyn owner Sir James Drummond Williams left the area to do a spot of peregrinating the place fell into disrepair and the parlour floors of the old mansion were reputedly turned over to the cultivation of mushrooms by some Polish tenants.

I watched some perky pied wagtails exploring the leftover tidbits at a roadsite picnic site. These are birds which have an intimate relationship with agriculture, often nesting in farm outbuildings and this is reflected in the number of Welsh names for the bird, There are at least eighteen, from *brith y fuches* through *tinsigl y gwys* to *shigwti*.

I reached Llansawel in time for lunch but although I had been told that there were three pubs in the village one seemed closed for good. This was the 1980 best kept village in Dyfed. The Swan Inn wasn't serving lunch so I munched on crisps and chocolate and watched a repeat showing of the previous evening's catastrophic start to the Melbourne grand prix. This village has a strong connection with Pantycelyn. The hymn writer kept a school here after losing his curate's post in Llanwrtyd Wells. He also found love, meeting Mary Francis who would become Mali his beloved wife. The place used to have a close connection with, of all places, Oxford. Two men of the parish, John Williams and Griffith Powell, became successive principals of Jesus college in the seventeenth century.

As I climbed I noted the quilting of fields – reminiscent of the paintings of John Elwyn who wove them into his work. This is a land of green and gentle undulation, although the green is often artificially coloured now with the land given huge injections of nitrogen. One farm I went past had an outbuilding full to the rafters with plastic sacks of fertiliser which promised an early boost for grass. There is a monotonous familiarity to so much of farmland, with a monoculture rye-gass, kept low by platoons of sheep, most resembling billiard table baizes. When I used to walk the Carmarthenhire hills as a young boy there were many small fields which were abundant with wildlife, with plants such as sundews, petty whin and Dyer's greenweed and there would be butterflies too – fritillaries fluttering by. Sometimes I would be lucky enough to hear the song of the grasshopper warbler, like a fishing line being reeled in from a damp thicket. But I'd be hard pressed to find one nowadays. Such damp habitats are preciously rare and, besides, over forty years of age you begin to lose the top end of the hearing range and so, even if a warbler was winding its song, I might not know it. But I can hear them in memory and for that I am very grateful. But so many of the these fields have been drained in the days when you could get a decent grant for improving agricultural land and brown fields and stretches of white moor grass are now uncommon. It is little wonder that the barn owl has become such a scarce item in the countryside. Small mammals need long grass in which to hide. Wiuthout the scurrying mice and shrews and voles there is nothing for the owls to neat. And so we lose a thread in the tapestry and it is all the poorer for it.

I wanted to press on to Rhydcymerau. I had been there before, but only in books.

The village is on the rim of the great forest of Brechfa and the plantations of sitka spruce stripped away the spirit of the community according to the eponymous poem by the Christian poet, Gwenallt. The poem starts arrestingly by declaring that the 'shoots of the trees for the third war were planted/in the soil of Esgeir-ceir and the fields of Tir-bach/by Rhydcymerau.' The poem then harvests warm and yeasty memories of the poet's grandmother with the 'skin of her face as yellow-withered manuscript/and the Welsh on her lips the Welsh of Pantycelyn.' Gwenallt's grandfather, a 'wanderer from the eighteenth century' is similarly conjured up as is his bard-uncle Dafydd and other poetic members of the family, enough to justify his describing them as a 'nestful of poets' From the domestic detailing the poem switches tenor in the last stanza, as a barrenness creeps like a dark shadow across the lives of the family and the village and on the trees are 'the carcasses of poets, deacons, ministers and Sunday school teachers/whitening in the sun/washed by the rain and dried out by the wind.'

To get to the village you follow the steep sides of Afon Melinddwr (Millwater River) and this was one of the most repulsive stretches of the walk because every few yards revealed dozens and dozens of discarded car tyres which literally rubbished the pleasure to be had from walking along the edge of the wood, gazing out to Lan Ddu Cilwenau on the other side of the gorge. There were mattresses too, and fridges and other white goods. There was enough flytipped litter to ruin my stomach and by the time I reached the edge of the village and Abernant, home of that other Rhydcymerau writer, D.J. Williams I was feeling sickened and angry. There is a plaque on the wall of the house but I heard some strident voices yelling in the garden outside and decided not to visit the house itself.

I meet D.J. Williams most days, as he stares out myopically from a painting by the Penarth artist Ifor Davies called 'Tân yn Llŷn' that hangs above the fireplace. The bespectacled D.J is standing next to Saunders Lewis and that big man Lewis Valentine in a work based on the now iconic photograph taken by J.E. Jones of the three men on their way to the Magistrates' court in Pwllheli in September 1936 after setting fire to the RAF bombing range in Penyberth.

D.J.'s book about life in Rhydcymerau, *Hen Dŷ Ffarm*, lovingly and lyrically translated by the poet Waldo Williams as *The Old Farmhouse* is plangent with memories and lyrical in its evocation of the rootedness of his family in *y filltir sgwar*, the square mile. His family he knows have lived here for four hundred years and in telling the story of his growing up, first in Penrhiw before moving at the age of six to the one-horsepower holding of Abernant is a portrait of a Wales now long gone, when a huge workforce of men and women worked the land , and stories were told around blazing hearths and carriers were knight errants and drovers blazed trails across the land.

In this simple classic we encounter the materially impoverished playwright Twm o'r Nant, fled from the bumbailiffs of Denbigh. Poor he certainly was. Here was a writer so skint that he used to make his own ink using elderberries. *Hen Dŷ Ffarm* also allows us to overhear conversation with Carmarthenshire natives who still use a Welsh which weaves in Demetian dialect, which derives from the ancient tribe which once encamped here. There are vivid vignettes of such people as D.J's grandfather who brought the first mowing machine to those parts. It also offers sobering statistics about the language. Writing in 1953 he points out that 'A hundred years ago four out of five of the people of Wales spoke Welsh. Now only one in three does.' Fifty years later the slide means that one in five people speak Welsh and the 2001 census might sound strident klaxon bells.

Williams has this to say about the habit of divesting 'ourselves of all national pride in things of our own and adopting grander foreign substitutes.'

> Take for instance, our Teutonic surnames, our Joneses, Evanses, Davieses, and Williamses and so forth, instead of ap Sion, ap Dafydd, ap Gwilym which no doubt came to be considered old-fashioned. (The Scot has never renounced his 'Mac' or his kilt on that score, nor the Irishman his 'O' or his accent.) . . . Take again the ostentatiousness of our business houses, our London houses and our Cambridge stores and our West End arcades, and the royal names we give our public houses, our Kings, our Queens, and our dukes of every shape and forms and our Lions of every colour.

Rhydcymerau itself offered plenty of evidence of Anglicization. The first house name plate I saw proclaimed pathetically on the front of a house – not a villa – 'Tony and Audrey, Orfa Villa' across the road from Red Dragon Parks with its 'holiday homes for hire, with on-site coarse fishing.' I stood outside Rhydcymerau chapel (built 1813; rebuilt 1874) and listened to the muted hymn singing that came from inside. There was a dessicated quality to the sound, like a language drifting – the words like crinkled leaves, the organ asthmatically keeping up.

I crossed Mynydd Llanybydder as the light began to fade. Dudley G. Davies's poem seemed apposite: 'Carmarthen hills are green and low/

And therealong the small sheep go/Whose voices to the valley come/ At eve, when all things else are dumb.'

The sheep hereabouts are special – this is Llanwenog country. It's a black-faced breed with a wool-tufted forehead which derived from the Shropshire Downs, although there is apocryphal talk about the line running back to the Cardi, or to a now extinct sheep, the Llanllwni which used to roam these hills. Though the breed takes its name from the parish of Llanwenog, the area where it evolved neatly coincides with the Y Smotyn Du, the so-called Black Spot. This was a term first used in the ninteenth century to describe a cluster of Unitarian chapel congregations in mid Ceredigion which proved resistant to the Methodist revivals which swept like wildfire through other parts of Wales. It was an area which was despised by those touched by the Holy Flame.

I arrive in Llanbydder in time to see the last lorries leaving the mart. Outside the Black Lion is a small farmers' market, the chatter of the stallholders a cheery, and for me, a cheering Welsh. As I leave the village a kite sweeps low over the road, showing off the russet in its wings.

You follow the meanderings of the Teifi on the next stretch which takes you past a school which has become the European Institute of Human Sciences. The village of Rhuddlan, a mile or so further, has seen a rash of English names break out on the face of the houses – Hazelmead, Rhuddlan Cottage, Pandy Cottage, Rhuddlan Mill, Y Graig Cottage and Lantern Lodge.

Large flocks of fieldfares chack angrily as I pass, unhappy about being disturbed as they rummage among the hedgerows. I pass an imposing motte and bailey castle above the village of Maesycrugiau and then cross the county line, between Ceredigion and Carmarthenshire at Llanfihangel-ar-Arth. You would develop strong calf muscles in this village which extends on both sides of the river with a very steep climb, enough to make villager turn mountain goat. Perhaps I exaggerate, or maybe it's the fact that if you're not used to it, a reasonable walk like this one can make your muscles hunger for oxygen or a damn good rest and the blisters attest to growing soft and pudgy in a life which is chair-bound. And I have been leading the city life, sitting before a computer, sitting in a car for too long. In fact this outing will probably be a turning point. At forty two you can't afford to allow your insides to fur up with fancy living. When I last saw Robin he dispensed some of his usual wisdom, but this time there was a sense of serious underlining of the words. He pointed out that ever since he started his first job he hadn't had time to think and it had taken his illness to give him time to mull-over and ponder. I knew he was offering this as a caution, because like Robin the work ethic is strong in me and I feel that I have a lot to do. But this walk, undertaken in memory, no, in the company of a special man, was a reminder that there is more to this experience of living than just the human. I learned more from Robin than ever I did in university and the generosity of a mentor often involves gifts you're not aware of being given.

There are few public footpaths in this part of Wales. So the last stretch is entirely on tarmac with the occasional thrill of being caught in the draught of a big truck as it really burns diesel. The air is still as I reach Llandysul, with its sewin-rich river meandering slowly, pink with evening. A huddle of youngsters gathers around the bus stop near the church, en route for a disco dance competition. An ancient language is on their lips, vivid and flawed. I wonder what the future holds. And hear their words falling like husks, to be swept up by the sweeper, whenever he comes.

CORACLES AND CROMLECHS

Osi Rhys Osmond

CORACLES AND CROMLECHS

Walking with, for, in memory of a man. Following the Teifi seawards.

Someone who joined me at the end of one day remarked, 'This is a very French river,' and I knew at once what she meant.

At Llandysul, alongside the church, the river saunters grandly, but it can quickly become capricious. It carves through the slate of its bed, the soft slate which allows chambers. Chasms and channels are engineered by high-falling water, heavy rains and rapid draining. Mortars are pestled, pebbles polished, grooves ground out in time.

Sometimes, gorged on rain, the river raises its skirts and spreads out over its banks and beyond, claiming more and making islands of long-rooted plants on spare beds of bare pebbles among trees who now have no security of tenure.

It has a gravitas, a seriousness, this river, but also a longing to lounge, to catapult, spray, speed up, narrow and change direction suddenly. It accelerates through dropping gorges, taking with it the evidence of its power. It hangs on to the broken remnants of branches and strands whole trees, large trees that have been torn up in the temper of its flood. It marks its temporary withdrawal from hastily-claimed, stretched edges, with dead leaves and crisp grasses, the desiccated tears of our wild river woods.

The river occupies its landscape, is the making of that landscape and its definition; it consolidates the land and measures how it lies. It grows trees and fells them. It fattens pastures and conditions cattle; sheep and horses sparkle on its lawns. It removes them, maroons them, drags them away and conceals them.

It collects and spreads chippings of its own making, it grades gravel in banks that lie resting, still. Staggering and quivering and silent almost, it moves glacially, storing sands. It mourns and meanders, slow and calm. Fat and flat and spread deep in places it is poised, perfect, superior, resolved never to hurry. But then, sucked down – slowly first, then drawn like rhubarb, faster, then with no control whatsoever – it descends by the first relentless, bevelling draw of bottomless attraction, to froth and dank oblivion.

LLANDYSUL: POETS, PREACHERS AND PRINTERS

Pensive with poets, saintly Llandysul sits silent by the Teifi, sliding down its bank. Between the forted tops, above the river's graded plain it hangs, a torc of terraces smiling on its hill. Gripped by roads and sustained by dwellings, transfixed by pubs and inns, articulated by stores, chapels, warehouses and old mills, this is home to poets of every gender, along with traders, printers, preachers, solicitors and bartenders. It has houses that could be museums, legal offices frozen in time and cafés steaming with tea and milky coffee. It is the great capital of stoves. Rayburns and all their glossy accessories assemble, patiently awaiting fitting, confidently anticipating decades of warm, homely glory in newly-converted, long farmhouse kitchens.

Old business gets done here with that certain, slow country walk; people meet and talk, and look into those same faces their ancestors saw, seeing their own past in other eyes. Talk is not so hurried; much has already been said, many years before, the even conversation of a continuing culture. The long-distance, ancestral relay race, with language, words and images passed on like batons, from generation to generation. Without tractors and electricity, free from gadgetry and tricks, they traded here and bought and sold; their suits were stitched and sewn, carts were made and wheeled away, animals marketed, stock replenished. Here tools were made, mended and replaced.

But now the car in all metallic, shiny promise proclaims Llandysul motor city, where Rovers and Skodas preen, smooth and shiny in the showrooms that avenue the southern entrance to the town. Others of more exotic pedigree await repair in shabby forbearance, under dragon signs: continental breeds, VW and Citroen, the eccentric accoutrements of ferreters, the moonlight steeds-to-be of lonely knights.

The pubs perform their welcoming and Pont Tyweli leaps across the Teifi's stream. Ceredig on his conquest paused here, and the river forms the moving frontier between his county, Ceredigion, and Sir Gâr. Arches soar and span in stone; arabesques and rococo swerves of road and river three-dimensionally contrive completion of a strange geometry. The river strains, restrained, directed, its power sent through narrow channels where once it spun wheels to make flour and fabric, wove and ground to something utile the grass and corn and wool and milk that careless rivers raise.

The town whispers to itself and down on the river's bank the church of Tysul squats and broods on time in placid slate and calm historic dignity. Inside is cool, and built this way in ordered rows, a church becomes a chilling space. Tysul came to the ford where passing trackways met and crossed, and here the town began, under the shelter of the hill. The original church was perhaps first established at Pencoed-foel, as a religious order, existing in seclusion, away from the main centre of population. Tysul: born 462 died 544, son of Corun and grandson of Ceredig, brother of Cenau, fourth Bishop of St Davids, Caranog and Pedr of Lampeter, and cousin of David our patron saint. The Welsh, as always, all related. Feast Day, January 31st.

There are murmurs in the walls, voices set in stone that have a tale to tell. Of Romans, Britons and of those who began to speak the liquid language, that now at last seems doomed to fade, slipping in silent increments from our forgetful lips, and less in oral evidence with almost every step.

There are strange words, carved in stone, VELVOR FILIA BROHO, speaking of ancient times. This is a shortened form of 'Velvoria the daughter of Brohomaglus', who is also recorded in the north, at Pentrefoelas, Denbighshire. There are other cut stones, sometimes abused – for cattle scratching, gate hanging, chimney spanning – lying far off as sills in sombre churches. The altar of the Lady Chapel holds a crucifixion carved in stone, with Christ, Mary and St John, which once looked down from the west tower, where it was fixed above the door. The altar stone is early and has incised Christian markings. Found on the slopes of Coed-foel, after being brought down to the churchyard and placed upright like a gravestone it was eventually brought in to serve as the altar stone, and dedicated in 1939. It is said to date from the foundation, so it may be one of the oldest in Wales. Outside the church, around the porch, are chunks of quartz, the baffling, ubiquitous mineral crystal, that decorates our sacred places. Silica the communicator follows our path; quartz is scattered everywhere and marks the route the pilgrims make.

On the former New Year's Day, the 12th of January, a feast was celebrated in Llandysul, which, it is said, generally deteriorated after mid morning into drunkenness as consumption became more liquid and less orderly. The ball was kicked, and heads as well, between teams from surrounding villages and parishes; rowdy sports that surely had their ancestry in older conflicts.

The Boats of Kidnapped Cultures

The river, hackles rising as it leaves the crouching town, is picadored with hanging lances, strung from taut nervous systems of zig-zagging strings.

For now canoeists jerk among its hidden rocks and ride its sullen channels spikily. Gaudy poles stab down and waver hesitantly in the air. Through slaloms of spume, not snow, the challenge set is to dodge and duck among strange currents, while sat in boats of other lands – kayaks, canoes; not coracles, whose passive, gentle disposition offers no thrills for those who seek a private war with water. Strange boats haunt the falling river now, and garish colours celebrate their presence with loud cries. Heads like 'Smarties' bob and bounce upon the stream and anoraks in sherbet shades of man-made fibres shriek and scream. Paddles quiver, rise and fall with speed to wound the running river and in promiscuous pleasure shove aggressively against the banks and rocks.

The ghosts of poachers, poets and river-watchers past shudder at this tumult. If all art aspires to be as music is, and culture too, here are the sounds of club-land thumping by. Finally, the boats of kidnapped cultures, born victoriously aloft and held by bungee-cords, head for home on trailers, vans and roof racks.

Once you could have a suit, or clogs made in Llandysul: now you can ride the rapids in a fibreglass canoe.

The river falls on down, changing mood and speed and dancing, surging, moaning, making the deep music that only river-water makes.

ANGELS AT HENLLAN

The road to Henllan skirts the river, pushing closer by the route-defying cliffs. The view is now breath-stealing as the river ducks and falls, but wait a moment for the turning, take your time and see it properly, in its strangely savage moods.

At Pont Henllan, pause to see the angels dancing. Cross the bridge of ancient arches. Leave the road, take the route back up the gorge, walk and move against the flow. Here the stranded alluvial gardens grow, landscaped by the bursting waters; crops of celandines and wood anemones, clumps of abandoned bluebells hover on exposed tree roots, in an instant archaeology of riverbank biology. Layers and segments lie exposed, bulbs and tubers loiter with displaced fecundity. The rocky channel's slated grooves and smooth worn edges change with every contour on the journey down.

The falls of Henllan are a place of prophecy, and angels sometimes visit, as they did to Sawdde, son of Ceredig, to speak of future greatness in his son, our Saint, whose birth was heralded to come 'mid thunder loud and flashing lightning'.

The prophesying Angel said, 'Tomorrow you will go hunting, and will get three things near the river Teifi, namely a stag, a salmon, and a swarm of bees in a tree above the river, at a place now called Henllan, which will belong to one who is not yet born, and he will own the two places, Linhenllan and Liconiuancan, until the day of judgement.'

The church of Henllan lies hidden in its hollow, thought to be dedicated to St David and on the site of a circular enclosure, close to the river and under a hill.

A blessed place, Henllan, and strange to see the wartime prison camp, in mean grey blocks, straddling the road and attempting as always to reinvent itself. The station at Henllan is now the tiny terminus of one of the toy railways of Wales. You can take a trip of several hundred yards and enjoy the romance of the days of steam in a narrow wooded valley. Welsh souvenirs decked out in all their vulgar glory, a Welsh lady as a tea-cosy, all the tools and relics of another time, put down, picked up and relished by those who never knew the real working days of steam. There was a time when Newcastle Emlyn trains were full of homespun suits and busy people, bursting with a sense of purpose, those who knew the value of direction and the need for destination. But now this track is the ultimate shunter's paradise, its locomotive afflicted by the stuttering gait of senseless travel: arrival, departure, arrival, reversal and arrival. Tea and Welsh cakes. Postcards. Departures, clutching souvenirs.

THE ANATOMY CLASS

The Teifi seems to be so anthropomorphic. Two lanky legs are laid out on the map, loosely connected at the hip by the rheumatic falls of Henllan. On either side, roads skirt the river and for county patriots the path can be in Ceredigion or Sir Gâr, or by river crossings, each in turn. Or follow the railway's course. A long bone runs through both these legs, once straight splints of steel. The railway tracks the river, hiding in tunnels when the gradient's steep. Between Llandysul where our journey starts and Cenarth gorge, before the Teifi falls, a right and left of lazy fertile land. Along two polarizing limbs the river wanders here and mostly gently flows, meandering from side to side in lazy curves, jig-sawing the county edges into a flat green puzzle.

A small spectacular at Pont Felin Cwrrws, where the Afon Cunllo sinks deep into a trench and the high bridge stretches itself to span the yawning gap. Decorated by an arcing avalanche of rotting fridges, and bejewelled by plastic debris, the banks plummet down, and clinging to them are garlands of shrubs, escapees from gardens, not prison camps. Way below, the narrow stream torrents along eager for the Teifi's breadth.

In Llandyfrïog, along the fruitful flooding plain, on a warm damp day, when all is still, sit, look and listen; you can hear and see the thick grass grow. The church of St Tyfrïog is now rebuilt and near here on a December morning in 1814 the last duel in Cardiganshire was fought. Heslop and Beynon had been drinking and in their cups they quarrelled. Heslop, who was Jamaican, and black, had been in a shooting party at Newcastle Emlyn. His complaints of poor sport due to the Cardiganshire gentry forbidding him the best positions turned into a quarrel. Beynon, a local solicitor, tried to calm the situation by remarking on the barmaid. This incensed Heslop, who, in protecting her honour issued a challenge, 'You, sir, are a scoundrel.' Walking away from each other on the river's edge, Beynon dishonourably, it is said, turned early, fired and Heslop fell, shot in the back. 'Poor Heslop', as he became known, is buried in the churchyard at Llandyfriog. Beynon, in disgrace, but freed by local justice went to ground, eventually leaving some time later for a new life in America.

The road from Llandysul to Pentre-cwrt, which has an inn, is there for those who want to drive and take their ease. It remains in old Sir Gâr, faithfully following the river, where it can. There are some public pathways marked, but they are not so simply shown as to make the walking tour straightforward, and the roads can be very busy. It is actually possible to follow the railway line in certain sections. There are plans to create a walk from Cardigan to Llandysul, but still too many stretches remain unresolved. Take the road to cross the river where the railway cuts through a narrow gorge between Bercoed Isaf and the old settlement of Henfryn. Past the mills the river plummets down the gap between the heights, the railway line becomes a road, and suddenly embarrassed, rushes on to fill the tunnel, deep below Bryn Teifi's hill.

The names along the river tell a story; they remind us, they remember what the older dwellers thought, and felt. Where the fat lands sit and second crops grow, the Dôl- prefixes old farm surnames: Dolhaidd, and Y Ddôl alone.

Pentrecagal is self-mocking in its name, evoking shock and wonder in a traveller – town of sheepshit? Where's the beauty? Where's the awe?

Down in Aberarad, past the one-time workhouse, flats and creamery, mozzarella scents the air. Newcastle Emlyn. Chapel and vestry, giants of good intention, flank the entrance to the town. Over on the Ceredigion shore, among evergreens fit for the Black Forest, the approach passes the castellated gateway to the estate of Cilgwyn.

APPLE-MACS AND MOZZARELLA

Fixed on a great tight bend of the river, sprawling across its plain and tumbling down from its low hills, Newcastle Emlyn, when approached

by the Cardigan road from Henllan, looks sleekly continental. The connection goes a long way back: the Romans were thought to have come and stayed and the name itself may come from the Roman Emilianus. Italian pizza and mozzarella manufacture now complete the chain. Newcastle Emlyn is and was a European town in Wales, and remains for the present among the most Welsh in language.

The town has an attitude, it has purpose, it belongs here, and mysteriously has a castle, but no mediaeval church. As an ancient border between church estates and private land across the river, it has grown in different ways, with history and events overtaking the two sides in turn. Adpar on the Ceredigion side has the remains of its own motte and bailey. An ancient borough at one time, it even sent an MP to Westminster. The earliest printing press in Wales was established here by Isaac Carter. The first publication appeared in 1718, *Cân o Senn iw hên Feistr Tobacco*. The press was moved down to Carmarthen about 1725, and Carmarthen became an important centre for the book production necessitated by the increased religious, intellectual and political activity of an awakening Wales.

In some ways Newcastle Emlyn is a new town, a comparative newcomer in the settlement stakes. The castle was built by Meredudd ap Rhys Gryg in around 1240, when he expanded his own territory to the south and took over the Commote of Emlyn. The castle was originally built as an administrative centre – not quite as romantic as the usual image of castles in Wales – for bureaucrats, rather than brave defenders and wild marauding bands. Passing between crown and local lords the castle finally came to ruin in 1648 when Cromwell's men demolished it by gunpowder. Like many other castles at that time it became a quarry, a supply of ready materials, a sort of masonic B and Q for local Sunday builders. The castle had a chapel which was dedicated to the Holy Trinity and it was here that the townspeople worshipped, hence the lack of an older church. Capel Bach y Drindod was built on the site in 1780 and became a National School, moving to a site near the present church in about 1863. The town now thrives in new ways: Antur Teifi (and lots of other adventures over the Teifi) sport an abundance of translators, antiques, mozzarella, Apple-Mac computers and wood-burning stoves, all complementing the stock utilities of a west Wales market town. You can still buy shoes here – another good test of economic vibrancy in any small place. Theatre, town hall and cattle market every Friday, early closing on a Wednesday. The town is spread out in parts, with streets wide enough to muster cattle and begin the drover's drive. And just to prove the vigorous town is well, in life and death, there's a large selection of respectable and well-advertised undertakers.

The park along the Teifi frames the river on its flat broad plain. Big trees stand unmoved and statuesque. A huge bow bends around the steep castle hill, like a pin brooching the town on its antique green cloak.

Conspiracies of picturesque desire are framed here by landscape backdrops that seem to urge themselves on us spectators as suitable subjects for our aesthetic contemplation.

A new path circles the park, marking it off in a defining line of proud civic jurisdiction. And if this part of the river forms a leg, the town sits in a very complex knee joint. From these comfortable meadows it is easy to see why this flat valley became the place to settle. On every hill and promontory you can witness just how much dispute there was as motte and fort, castle and settlement symbols dot the map. These mute reminders tell of older times when power changed and violent endeavour shaped the land and people. The castle fragments punctuate the place, holding in order the sprawling town, while under its side runs the river, held by the weir, then sent tumbling down across the jagged slate beneath the bridge and on towards Cenarth. The mill-race siphons off a section, turned from dancing fury to silky calm in yards. The race is wide and deep and strong; it turned once the wheels of the mill, high above the frothing waters. That mill made electricity, like so many of the west Wales flannel factories – sometimes for their own use and very often for the benefit of the local population. Alternative energy is old news in these parts.

CWM-COU TO CENARTH: WATERFALLS AND CORACLES

Below the bridge at Newcastle Emlyn the river riots, side to side, in twists and turns; it charges through its narrow channel and pours along and then calms down. We can follow the road, as ever – not the most attractive route – or there are paths on the Sir Gâr side.

We're moving down now along the lower limb, the shin-bone of our lovely river's leg. Strange names abound: Cwm-cou across the river on the Ceredigion shore where Felin Geri ground the corn, packing healthy eating, wholesome wholemeal, with millstone grit and speckled flour. Back on Sir Gâr's sheltered flank, flourish Gillo Fach and Gillo Farm, Gelli Gatti and Allt Gelli Gatti, Italian endings one and all. Under the trousered trees of Corduroy Wood sits Barnet, sad and lonely, far from home. Soar Farm is not a chapel, nor the smallest sinful city, dehydrating on the plain, nor a hot place, sandy desert, lowest spot on Lot's poor earth. Just a farm in biblical Cymru, non-conformist from the start.

The gorge above Cenarth stands steep, the river charges wildly on, the scrub oaks cling, their toenails curling as they strain to grip the shallow, tilting earth. The geology, in mean upheaval, refuses burial, it surfaces and challenges the old supremacy of soil, dislodging trees and clumps of flowers, ferns and fungi, senselessly risking its own rocky balance, it falls, a flaky flood of shale. While slowly, stately, salmon-holding Teifi gently changes, becomes the object of adoring admiration, photographed and painted, pirouetting through its paces, flouncing, pouting, splashing down.

The falls fall, the bridge spans, the shops smile, enticingly. The weir and fish traps train the river, water dressage, ordered gravity in fluid form. Llawddog, river architect and saint, built fish jumps, liquid ladders that assist the salmon's compelling urge to spawn. The mill, the National Coracle Centre, and falls, spectacular twisting dives, huge stone steps split the river across its slate-bedded stage. The sudden dislocation of geology permits the plunging water its moment of scenic glory. Foaming arabesques race down, pools whirl, while eddies swirl, hover, fade, drawn sinking to the bottomless dark.

The falls and salmon fishery once supported a large community and Gerald of Wales was impressed by the richness of the fishery and by the orchards and mills of Cenarth when travelling around Wales to draw up support for the second crusade in 1188.

The present bridge was designed by the Edwards family of Pontypridd in 1787, and is clearly a related design to their masterpiece on the Taff, with its circular holes lessening the load of the supporting arches, and occasionally the river pours through them in dramatic sprays of wild flood water. Glimpses of river scenery and downstream greenery are framed through spans and spheres, while the road soars above, aloof from surrounding commerce and commotion. There's a grandstand view of weir and waterfalls and below us all those people picking paths across the slippery slate, risking decorum for sober exploration. Camera bearers make mini expeditions to exposed positions, seeking superior vantage points to snap and frame, to still or capture the movement that excites.

Cenarth sprawls across the road and river, pinned by the bridge and brightly painted in new season's sun, with bated breath keenly awaiting its new and old admirers, wearing full make-up and enticing signs. Florid hanging-baskets swing erotically, like pendant ear-rings dangling from the oddly-coloured head of a revitalised sex worker. The eager expectancy of tourist trade, the exchange of currency, the sharp shriek of clamouring tills, all conspire to undermine what was. What is tradeable from our past? And what can be our new commodity? How are the antiques pasteurised, disinfected and made clean? Just how are the unexploded bombs of people, places, cultures, defused and rendered harmless, souvenired?

The lower falls spill out into a spinning, placid pool, where sometimes coraclemen fish by star signs, and tourists squander time, lost in travellers' reverie.

St Llawddog's Well waits for watermen. His church looks out from the high ground, across the motte, over the roofs, past bridge to chapel, beyond the old toll-gate to the steeply wooded hills and along the broadening valley. Through lowered eyelids, it looks at the village, embarrassed by its flirty brazenness.

Close to the south door of the church the conical standing stone of Gellidywyll protrudes through the earth of the graveyard. Ice-worn and inscribed CURCAGN– FILI ANDAGELL– (Curcagnus, son of Andagellus), this is an upended missile from an age of stone. It was moved from Gellidywyll in 1896 at the instigation of Lord Cawdor; local tradition claims it originally stood near the church, at Parc Maen Llwyd, before being removed to form the memorial stone for the favourite horse of a militia captain. Other stories associate the stone with Maenclochog, where it was said to have stood by the roadway next to a house known as Bwlch y Clawdd. Another stone at Llandeilo near Maenclochog has the name Andagellus inscribed in ogam, so there may be a connection.

Inside the church, restored, like so many in the district during Victorian times (in this case by Sir Gilbert Scott), there stands a very unusual font, unremarkable in itself, but the bowl tells another intriguing story of misuse, reclamation and rededication. Used as a pig trough after being removed from its original home in the parish of Llandysiliogogo, it was recovered by a former vicar of Cenarth and placed in the church. A serpent-like band circles and loops around the font bowl and at three points there is a human face in low relief, while at the fourth loop there is a double face, just like a Celtic Janus figure. Vigorous in design and execution, but fairly primitive, it suggests an early date, certainly pre-mediaeval.

Saint Llawddog himself is said to be a descendant of Nedd Hael, a prince of northern Britain who settled in the area during the coming of Cunedd Wledig in the sixth century. The early Celtic church, being monastic in structure, operated the same marketing methods as MacDonalds, setting up and expanding its influence outward by franchise. Llawddog established the original monastic foundation at Cenarth and eventually became the patron saint of the district, which celebrates his feast day on the 24 of January. Llawddog would find the village very similar in size, shape and layout today, but might have some communication difficulties with many of the present population.

The Norman motte, on the rise opposite the church, constructed to defend the strategic vantage point of the river crossing was thought to be the home of Nest, the daughter of Rhys ap Tewdwr, and the wife of

Gerald of Windsor. Reputed to be the most beautiful woman of her time and known as the Helen of Wales, she inflamed all who saw her. Having been the mistress of Henry I, by whom she already had a child, she was desired by her cousin, Owain ap Cadwgan. Disregarding propriety and senseless with passion he tunnelled under the gate of her husband's castle at Cenarth Bychan, which burned to the ground in the attack, and, with her apparent contrivance, stole the beautiful Nest away to Irish exile.

CWM CYCH: CARAVANNING WITH PWYLL

The road to Abercych meets the river at Glandŵr and then heads on up the hill between Allt Ceiliog and the wooden, holiday chalets of Penlan Village, which glowers in spruce-scented Nordic melancholy on its lonely Welsh hill. The deciduous edges of the pinewood on the steep, twisting road down are filled with flowers, flying litter and singing birds, but the traffic is fast and frequent. It is possible in dry weather to take a more adventurous high path through the woods on the right, where the road rises at Glandŵr. The route passes above the meeting point of the two rivers and descends to cross a ford and join the road above Abercych. Before we cross the bridge to Abercych we pass a lorry graveyard.

There was a ferry here once, across the little Cych. The Nag's Head Inn with its cautionary biblical text, '*bydd graff fel sarff, diniwed fel colomen*' ('be crafty like a snake, innocent like a dove') guards the entrance to the secretive Cwm Cych, where Pwyll of Mabinogion fame pursued his quarry. Pwyll might have enjoyed the mythological mix of marsh marigolds and the hordes of six-berth caravans facing us – displaced suburbia, terraced in rows across the stream.

Dreams are expressed on roads in Wales, in self-doubting, proudly home-made signs: 'Fly fishing', 'Riding', 'Ponies' sing their sad songs of urban longings.

The route now strikes against the current and the river rises as we turn back on ourselves to face the east. The Cych is small but complete, with all the vocabulary of bigger flows, and it has its own tricks. Tumbled trees across its banks are home to hanging gardens on their horizontal backs. The river swings and fattens, narrows and pours, carves islands and deposits peninsulas, it civil engineers sandy bank perpendiculars, holed like edam, high rises for river life. Kingfishers flash fast in natural neon and puritan dippers duck and rise, dunking themselves like obsessive Baptists. Avenging complacent geology, Afon Cych has a new agenda, moving shingle and grading by stranding gravel, sand and composting leaves and branches. A tiny, model Amazon, festooned with ivy and garlanded with ferns. At Glandulais lane a sunken wall strides low along the riverbed, under the bridge and out the other side, and a golden butterfly, with brown eyes on her wings, leads on.

Choose your flower season for this walk, schedule botanically by bluebell, wild garlic, primrose, celandine, violet and foxglove. Select a hazel pilgrim staff, taken best in cold December and sap-free January.

The house of Lancych, grand and languid, where pheasants call, has leafy lawns leading down to gravelled driveway splendour. There are old beech trees of heroic size, and, all alone, a druidic, actor's oak, astray from Dunsinane. Huge walls and stables, coach houses and yards are the abandoned assembling points of servant-intensive, country estate domestica. Pont Glan Cych is crumbling now, and quartz glistens gnomically, fallen in field gateways. This way for Caws Cenarth, but the road fails, so turn back up the hill out of Cwm Cych and climb up steeply towards Bwlch-y-groes.

ARARAT AT Y FRENNI FAWR

To follow the river along its valley, pacing the descent to the relentless rightness of water falling, is to metronome the rhythm of one's stride. Now the swift shock of gradient as we climb creates new pleasures and alarms. The head moves faster, in rapid jerks, as views are snatched and glimpses stolen, other perceptions dawn in the breathless rising of the road. Large houses, laid out generously like expensive toys, look out loftily from their vantage points. Ffynone, home of Earl Lloyd George, looms larger in foreshortened exaggeration than the whole village of Capel Newydd, straggling sparsely along, beyond the ridge.

Mrs Rita Evans, Rhyd y Frenni, whose film star name and friendly face impress, tells in Preseli Welsh the tale of Star, the village tucked below the road in the tight valley of the Cneifa. Her handsome husband walks on, supported by his stick, a Bogart to her Hayworth. In Star, a heavenly light shone down one night as the minister walked to preach the chapel service.

At Clydau, sign-posted, but missing from my map, the round yarded church has old secrets hidden and the narrow lanes enclose, unexpectedly, Hoseasons Holidays in a large and ancient farmhouse. St Clydau was the daughter of Brychan Brycheiniog, and in the west wall of her church are three remarkable stones. The first is dedicated to St Salirius, who came here from Gaul in 431 AD. St Edern, who is represented on the second, arrived from Donegal and the ogam and Latin inscription reads ETERNI PHILI VICTOR. The third stone, Dugoed's Stone, so called because it was found on the farm of that name, close to where the road left Cwm Cych, is inscribed with a cross inside a circle, and is also likely to have an Irish connection. There are three steps in the north wall, leading to the *lloft y grog* (rood-loft) where the priest would say mass for the souls of the dead, enabling them to leave purgatory more speedily. Here is material evidence of the evolution of the Church in Wales, through Celtic, Catholic and now to Anglican worship.

Pathways pattern the map, vague embroideries picking out their well-worn ways. Fittingly, at Garreg Wen, the largest upright chunk of quartz on our journey stands guard, resonating brightly with its mystic powers. Climb up to whinberry-picking altitude and the names take on new meanings – Casgwynt, Cefn Croes – and scowling dogs and lurid plastic toys flower the yards of grey farms. The empty, abandoned school is a haunting shell, ringing with the lost language of ghostly children.

'Inglenook' would seem incongruous at Bwlch-y-groes, where the pilgrim route darts between chapel and store, and across the crossroad, more quartz. The chapel graveyard laid out in old expectancy is now half full, as though someone had accurately assessed a culture's need to die, forecasted occupancy and decline with precision. '*Bois y Frenni yn dawel heno*', although, remember, the first Urdd singing school was held here, at Bwlch-y-groes, in 1940.

The rising fields stiffen with short grass growing on a mean covering of thin soil, cropped spring-close by ewes and rams, and bounced upon, a great green trampoline, by celebrating Easter lambs. Trees abscond, hedges shrivel and gorse epaulets the hills and promotes in rank the curving ridges. On the slope of Y Frenni Fach, sheep process in patient line, stringing the lower fields in long woolly skeins. The Frenni are named, it is claimed, from their resemblance to upturned boats, *brenni*, their silhouettes the keel and prows. The name is now displayed in foreign fields by flag-decked juggernauts of Frenni Transport. The name of sacred hills speeds down motorways and sails across seaways on saintly ferries, contemporary routes of commercial pilgrimage.

Beneath Y Frenni Fawr a farm, appropriately a tiny Ararat, caught high in the moor's grip, has a boat alongside, a ship stranded dry and far from sea, with sun-swallowing Cardigan Bay gleaming longingly in its western sight. The tumuli on top look down, and from an infantry of fir, they frown on everything below.

FOEL DRYGARN: A STONY CANAVERAL

The road to Crymych drops. Pace the walk to meet suns falling. Put the glow behind Foel Drygarn. Schedule to illuminate the grandeur, and choreograph your view. The sharp road between Y Frenni Fawr ribbons downwards, and way behind the bowl where Crymych basks, Preseli proper rises in pagan incredulity, presided over in triangular drama by the stone-decked pyramid of Foel Drygarn.

The pubs were closed, the chip shop bare, but ironmongeries sparkled in rude health, another sure sign of cultural vigour. Meat and hairstyles, drugs and medicines, antiques, a school, a pool, a garage selling books and diesel, but best of all, 'Bwyd y Byd' (Food of the

World), local necessity and imported delicatessen luxury, announced and served in Welsh. An abundance of bars, blocks, fruits and nuts and drinks to quench and power our upward climb.

The road leaves the village and heads for Mynachlog-ddu, to where pilgrims in earlier times might have diverted to worship with the Black Brothers from which the parish takes its name. The road enters the National Park and soon we leave the tarmac and join the track, in a lost lane, a cultural landscape valve. We cross the stile and ease ourselves into this wild and timeless place. Tradition claims that the right of common pasture dates from grants made to the sons of Cuhelyn by the Norman Lord of Cemais. We are now entering the enchanted land, where huge assemblies of sacred stones and ancient sites await, spun out across the moors, silent and sentient. The climb ahead offers the freedom to cross open ground with no restraints – though at first comes the cautionary notices to the geological souvenir hunters of bluestones, robbers of birds' nests and plunderers of plants. The turf is lachrymose, weeping as it takes a walker's weight. At certain contours springs leach, drying the bogs that cross our path. The draining streams, Welsh wadis, each carves a tear duct through the moor, exposing peat, bright earth and yellow-stained stones. Other distant walkers, scattered, vivid like sweetwrapping litter, dot the isolated hills. The mountain ponies, perhaps adherents of Epona, loiter, grazing lazily; they bear the marks of ancient praise and feel themselves, in truth, the only rightful occupants. The upward path is clearly seen, laid out above the ridgeway, with only small areas of treachery beneath our feet, but don't stop, don't look back or down or out; save it, invest in two kinds of future breathlessness.

THE SUMMIT: FOEL DRYGARN

From high among the aerial rocks of early graves, the world spreads out, below, above, in front, on every side: the moors, the fields, the woods, chapels, valleys, farms and distant cliffs and inlets to the sea. Spacemen in encircling satellites have no more cause to swoon, while we earthbound astronauts are moved and overcome. Now flight seems possible in our breathless state, eyes panting, focus failing, gazing, gulping, drinking down the cloudless view.

The three-cairn summit crumbles and scatters downwards, screes of boulders sprawl, graded gravitationally in order of descending size. Hard, stony seeds of future archaeology. Ground like pepper, shaken out, they punctuate the hill and swarm like angry insects stilled. Enclosures and hut patterns surround the summit. Foel Drygarn, enclosured, re-visited, re-built, re-occupied; *cartref*, home and burial place.

The land around is bleak and melancholic, to earlier pilgrims fearful and alarming, unmapped and mined by monoliths. The worshipper of many gods, or one, might hasten, nervously aware of frail appeasements made. West along the curving, arching ridge the dragon's back of mountain bones protrude and peaty earth falls back as though the skin is shrinking felt, hung like the pelt of some unrealised monstrous beast, toppled on its flank. Huge stones rear up like climbing glacial sheets, cubist ice-fields of stone collide in freeze-frame imagery, slabs shear off, tilt and fall in perfect archaeological symmetry. How much is nature and what is nature rearranged?

Volcanic activity contrived to create conveniently shaped and solid stones, the ready-made materials of landscape poetry. This is the place to build megaliths, construct tombs, defend oneself, retreat, admire. To sit and be, and scan the rimmed horizon, the hills and seas, and watch for enemies advancing or wave off departing friends.

And what if all of history's walkers came along in just one day? Early tomb-makers, cosmic worshippers, lunar and solar luminaries, possibly even troops of post-crucifixion Romans, striding the ridges, put carelessly out of their strict formations by geology and greed, nervously ransacking burial sites in search of mythic treasures. Missionary Christians making peace with redundant idols and learning to share new gods with old. Monastic saints and wandering hermits lost in prayer and deep in thought, meditating in high solitude. Caravans of pilgrims convoyed in piety, passing along the sacred way. Many-peopled presences, patrols of pensive spirit-seekers and military guardians, ever watchful. Modern hikers, SAS yompers, lovers, star-crossed and otherwise, mountain bikers, crystal gazers, National Park rangers, pony trekkers,

New Agers, archaeologists, naturalists, conservationists and geologists, shepherds, World War pilots, ley-liners, ornithologists and herders, dowsers, farmers, crashed hang gliders, grazers, poets, painters and unsuccessful bluestone movers. Histories here mount up like the cascading, frozen stones.

Carn Meini: Bluestones and Waldo

Conspiracies of dry grasses gossip as we step, and reedy voices Babel deep beneath our feet. We launch in grounded horizontal swoop towards Carn Meini. Across, above the springing moor the skylarks climb to touch the sky in sharp insistent song. The bogs are bottomless and hard to see, the intermittent path is vague and crosses dry peat carpets, powdered like discarded coffee grounds. Winds beat a rapid staccato as my notebook pages flap. A hawk marks out the sky, and maps the mountain monuments in complementary flight. Erratic ravens croak, flop and spin, calling out the names of megaliths and settlements of stones: Garn Ddu Fach, Carn Ferched, Carn y Ddafad Las, through the sheep fold, past Carn Gyfrwy to Carn Meini, from where, four thousand years before, some bluestones were moved mysteriously to southern plains, to cap Stonehenge. Carn Meini: the quarry grave where disrobed rocks outcrop to form the polar star in this stark fallen constellation of sacred summit sites.

On Good Friday I ate my lunch perched high on a flat-backed rock, the gold-marked butterfly passed by, and the currants on my Easter bun stared back, two deep, brown, familiar eyes, vigilant on a hill in Wales.

Below, on Rhos-fach common, is Waldo's tall, standing-stone memorial, connecting, tugging time and spreading out the Quaker poet's words of peace and brotherhood across mountain of his boyhood.

Foel Drygarn, Carn Gyfrwy, Tal Mynydd

Angry giants, warlike legendary heroes and gentle saints: stones allegorically hurled from here give meaning to unexplainable events and names to nameless things. Arthur, Samson – these are their quoits and javelins, tossed in anger or in jest. Peripatetic stones have strolled to bathe, and wandered out alone at night, while others have been re-appropriated, in kindly or cruel misuse. There is no shortage of legend in these parts.

Cairns appear along contours from Carn Meini to Carn Breseb, debris ranges from scattered stones to massive, sunken lumps of luminous quartz. Under Carn Alw, with its coarse file of *cheveaux de frise* still toothily intact, is a map of miniature worlds, of fat white farms, the chambered tomb of Bedd yr Afanc and islanded Hafod Tydful. Pilgrims may pass by Bedd Arthur, grave of our star-named hero, who has more resting places than a resurrected cat might need; then on to Carn Bica, and down the slope to rise on Mynydd Bach between the mounted warriors of Cerrigmarchogion. Along and up towards Foel Feddau, shadowed by Foel Cwmcerwyn and down to Bwlch Pennant, looking out over scooped-out landscape, the place the glacier stole away. Down the gulley, in a very necessary detour, a path descends through the standing sentries of pine to Rosebush, quarry ghosts and Tafarn Sinc. Brightly painted, and proudly expensive now, the quarry workers' cottages gleam from their terrace. The quarry pond is deep and cold. In the probing tunnels, fern-fronted and curtained by hanging moss, roofs seeping, the sound is the incessant, dripping plucking of the troglodyte's damp harp.

Working levels form stages in the sky and buzzards shift on their ledges, while jackdaws quarrel sociably. The buildings stand roofless and only the stubborn stones remain; all else fades and falls. Rosebush is re-colonised, resilient with post office and teas.

The Tafarn Sinc is a peopled *Marie Celeste* of a pub; in some ways it is as it was, Welsh-speaking, compromising itself only in self-interest and defence – it has modernised itself with sawdust, and hung cured hams in its hair. Outside, make-believe trains give off ventriloquists' steam in extra static frustration, as frozen Edwardians stand immobile to entertain the tourists.

The ridge we traversed is dark above, long and silhouetted, dotted with old stones and mounds. The ageless enormity of the view, is such that it seems to be more than simply the sum of its physical parts. What other, more metaphysical substance might these hills contain?

Cwm Gwaun to Nevern: Hanging Gardens and Holy Wells

The station stays, the route moves on, back through the pines, up past quarries to Bwlch Pennant and along the forestry track to Bwlch y Gwynt. Under Foel Eryr, look down and out across the well-laid table of the catchment of Afon Gwaun. Through Waun Trallwng Bog to Pen-lan-wynt, there is a bridle path to take. After Berth Gwynne the pilgrim has three interesting choices: follow the Afon Gwaun or the tracks and road to Fishguard, turn up the river and make for Nevern, or head south through Puncheston and Casnewydd-bach to join the major pilgrim route at Mathry.

However, to the serious pilgrim – and is there any other kind? – Nevern and its mysterious church should be considered an essential destination. Although there may be simpler ways of reaching Nevern than picking your way up Afon Gwaun, there are rewards for taking the river route. In upper Cwm Gwaun are hanging gardens of ferns in semi-tropical fecundity, nature being inclined to excess in these sheltered woods. There are holy wells and gardens, natural and man-made, nature trails, monuments, birds and flowers, old earthworks and stones. Cross the watershed between Afon Gwaun and Afon Clydach and there are places that can be discovered only from the air: strange, newsworthy names, experimental homes, contemporary round huts, settlements, instant archaeologies. Brithdir Mawr, Constantinople and New England hide among the trees.

Carn Ingli, where the Angels appeared to pious, tormented St Brynach, founder of Nevern, is skirted and surrounded by historic sites, indecently crowded with standing stones, cairns, circles and enclosures. It has treasure in abundance, could become a national asset, an open-air gallery of pre-history. There are enough relics to furnish any new country just starting out and without an ancient history of its own.

The summit of Carn Ingli forms an equilateral triangle with Nevern and Pentre Ifan and the route bisects the two great monuments. Down the valley the road over Pont Nanhyfer leads to the church of St Brynach, where the yew trees bleed Christ's blood and ogham stones stand sentinel or loll as window sills. The church and its environs form an enigmatic spot where much is hidden, as if some cryptic treasure hunt has been set out among the stones.

The first cuckoo calls in early April, from the cross of Brynach.

The cross of Nevern, almost 14 feet high, carved in local dolerite, is said to date from the tenth or early eleventh century AD, although that is debatable and its origins could be earlier, some feel. The patterns intertwine and weave, innocent swastikas are seen among the endless strands of stone, and letters depicting *Dominus*, from DNS, a shortened form of the Latin for 'Lord'. Made in two parts, with a join at the shoulder, it registers the change of function of standing stones from old pagan to new Christian use. A smaller, older stone names VITALIANI/ EMERETO, backed up by ogam script along the side, stands near the porch, while from the walls strange heads look down. Inside, the pews are decorated by a host of embroidered prayer cushions, in WI aesthetic, with nods to Celtic forms and William Morris. Those who come to old-tongue Wales can join the church and feel at home, while more foreign-sounding chapel daunts. Sewing oneself into a history and a place is a simple and popular means of apparent belonging.

A sill is carved in the form of an interlaced cross, an intriguingly simple design, a continuous ambiguous snaking line, marking out a figure or a cross, or both. Another sill stone acts as a fifth-century Rosetta, deciphering the ogam script by the Latin words alongside, a talking point for curious children. These stones, too, have been abused, have strayed and wandered from their work, taken up temporary positions and been fairly recently recovered and restored to other tasks. Memorials to great local men – landowning, historic, literary and medical – gaze down respectably.

Outside, a path leads through the cottage garden, over the stone slab bridge across the stream and on up the pilgrim's way to the wall or rocky face that is said to hide relics of the Holy Cross. The motte and bailey squats aloft, with a deep rock-cut ditch, squabbled over by natives and Normans. The trees and woods around are ancient and dramatic, vaulting the natural sacred site. A cross is picked out in the rock face and other crosses appear to those who search and stare. A kneeling step is carved, low down. Kneeling, I note a great solemnity descends on all around: this is a special place.

Above the trail a climb of footprints, time-worn, groove deep into the rocky ledge – a place to pray, meditate, or make small peregrinations, some have claimed.

And then the golden butterfly flew by, with two intense peat-brown eyes, shining darkly from its wings.

THE WORLD IN TUNE

Christine Evans

THE WORLD IN TUNE

Stand at the crossroad and look.
Ask for the ancient paths
and where the good way is.
Walk in it
and you will find rest for your soul.

Jeremiah, 6.16

SEIZING THE DAY

No ceremony at the parish boundary, no cross-led procession or sprinkling with holy water. Michael Fish's forecast of a change in the weather, even a few dry days, is enough: a couple of hours later, I am on the road.

Such a time of year for a journey, the medieval pilgrim in my head scoffs. Who ever heard of a February start? Don't you remember your Chaucer? 'Whan Aprille with his shoures swete . . . THAN longen folke to goon on pilgrimages.' Not February with his floods and bitter gales.

I know, I know. But in place of a letter from my lord of the manor, I carry an editor's instructions, and have an obligation to complete this 'pilgrimage' and write it up before the end of March. There were twenty-seven Severe Weather warnings last weekend, it has been the wettest February since the eighties, but time is running out. And, yes, I am aware that anything I do will be a mere travesty – loading up the Renault being nothing like setting off on foot, with a couple of days' bread and cheese and a spare pair of hose in your scrip. Hope my wellies are still in the boot. Waterproofs, woolly hat – won't need anything broad-brimmed to keep the sun off. But I have chosen suitable muted colours – brown and green. I've forgotten a stout stick, though. For vaulting over streams and beating off wild dogs and outlaws, naturally.

On the seat beside me, the large-scale map of north Pembrokeshire and a B&B guide. It has crossed my mind that travelling without a map would be much truer to the experience, though not as drastic as setting off in a boat without oars and trusting to Providence.

Just to set off is to silence doubts. I've demurred for weeks, as a double outsider – I don't know Pembrokeshire, nor am I a church-goer of any denomination. I'm not sure what to do in a church, haven't the vocabulary. (What is a pyx, anyway?) Am I even a Christian except by default? I can't imagine being committed to any organisation that claims exclusive access to the truth of things. I can be intensely moved by the language of the Old Testament, liturgical music, and shared silence, but I have no interest in a self-absorbed quest for an afterlife, and since I grew out of teenage mysticism, no faith in a creator with a personality.

So – will following old pilgrim paths be a trespass, visiting their churches and scrutinising their shrines an intrusion? On the other hand, I would like to make a spiritual journey; to set off without knowing exactly where it may lead and what I might find. In the end, remembering Dorothy Rowe's advice on how to cope with depression, I've decided to *behave as though* I believe, and see how it turns out.

To end up in St Davids. 'A few days . . . or as long as it takes,' is what I tell them as I set off.

I leave Llŷn still dark under a sodden wadding of stratus, Dolgellau swept by sleety blizzards, thunderclouds over Traws and the Dinas Mawddwy landscape looming and sinister as a Doré etching. The bridge over the Dyfi is under water, a combination of tidal surge and the south-westerly gales of the last three weeks, so I have to drive up the valley and round. Just before Cemmaes I see the first road-kill badger. Someone has dragged it clear and laid it carefully by the hedge with its head couched on its front paws, white blaze clear, startlingly like a sheepdog alert to the oncoming traffic. Soon after there's a fox, spread-eagled like a cartoon animal, and a second badger. A ragged broken bundle, drenched-dark, it is still hunched in the middle of the road on a stretch too busy to stop, and on a bend just before the Llangrannog turning is a third. This one has been flung to the side, probably by impact with a heavy vehicle, and tumbled upside down, those clever and powerful hands upturned and open to the rain.

'February, fill the dyke/Whether black or whether white.' It can only get better. It's not snow, and the days are lengthening.

THE WAY THROUGH THE TREES
(Nevern, Bayvil, Carni Ingli to Goodwick)

The sky is clear to the south. I begin to enjoy the shapes of the hills, of the trees in their still-undressed state, gentler greens. I crane over the steering-wheel to watch buzzards wheeling, and a single red kite – the excitement almost of a foreign country.

It's not remembering Nevern's ancient carved stones, but the map's deep green curve in the shadow of Carn Ingli that entices me off the main road. So down the hairpin bends into the valley, morning light tangled in the woodland on my left and the sound of the river below. A tatter of leaves hang on roadside oaks, the woods given perspective by scattered conifers and holly against which cascades of hazel catkins glitter as if sprayed with gold. Past the sign for Coedwynog Holsteins, ('Orders for Christmas geese taken now') and Rhydofferiad (The Priest's Ford) the valley broadens and levels into a wide green pasture, a real *maes-yr-haf* spreading out below the church. Surely in the Middle Ages it would have had fairs and festivals, dancing or Sunday games spilling over from the churchyard, wrestling or perhaps even *cnapan*, that early rugby described by the local Elizabethan historian George Owen: young men stripped to the waist wearing leather aprons and tackling for possession of a wooden ball slippery with pig's fat.

I sit drinking coffee from my thermos, letting the sound of birds and a small singing stream rinse the hiss of the miles from my ears. There's the constant small background chatter of chaffinch and robin and sparrow, blackbirds, what might be a nuthatch whistle, woodpigeons in the yews behind me. Cloud shadow ebbs and flows over Carn Ingli, rising steeply across the valley. For twenty minutes on a workday morning there's not a single car. Or tractor – it's probably *amser te deg*, or elevenses as they might call it here.

It's here that I first feel that stretching of time that comes from not having to be anywhere or answerable to anyone. A blissful buoyancy that comes to characterise this journey. It is a little like the dimension of a different language, the way you find yourself saying things you had not felt the need to express in your own – a release of unexpected slants and nuances. Nobody knows who I am or what my preoccupations, dreams and insecurities are. I could be anyone; or who

I am, only more so. Not mother, child, wife or teacher. All I need will be on my back or in the boot of the car just walking distance away.

A little uphill path leads me by chance into the top of the graveyard so I approach my first church from the back, missing the impact of the avenue of huge old yews towards the massive square tower. Like a castle; it reminds me that the church was rebuilt when Nevern was a Norman stronghold in the eleventh century. Inside is warm and welcoming and amber. Shadows cast by the trees outside ripple slowly as if we're underwater. I am overawed by the arching space, the elegant pointed windows and vaulted ceiling. *God's echoing house of shadowed arches.* To my left through a pointed arch is a big four-paned window and a staircase to the belfry.

A notice board by the door gives clues about the community. As well as the list of Lent services and flower rotas, there's a notice about a talk to be given by a farmer from South Africa and reminders: 'If you haven't already filled in an electoral form please do so and return as soon as possible'; 'John and Hilary are collecting the following to take to Romania in March – toothpaste, tampax, hair bands, notelets, biros . . .'

An embroidered wall hanging shows Brynach Sant by the stream, a hare crouched at his feet, flowers, a wooded valley and Carn Ingli's distinctive peak behind him. I'm surprised not to see the cuckoo that is supposed to have sung from the Great Cross on his deathday and every April 7th since. His tunic is a bit like Nain's bedspread, but the thing is remarkably finely done. I'm glad to find postcards of it, and of the kneelers that light up the nave with celtic crosses, triangles, triskeles and other motifs in Mediterranean colours – glowing greens and gold, crimson, ultramarine and purple.

I move slowly round the stretched cross-shape, studying the memorials. There are many Bowens of Llwyngwair; many young women and infants. After a while I find I am reading 'A Monument of Parental Affection' aloud in a hushed voice. It seems a fitting acknowledgement. I speak louder, enjoying the acoustics, the sonorous vowels.

In a stone-vaulted side chapel is a brass tablet to George Owen of Henllys, whose *Description of Pembrokeshire* I've just read in Gomer's Welsh Classics series. And here on the window sill is the long stone slab with irregular notches on the edge and large letters roughly cut:

MAGLCVNI FILI CLVTOR. Magloclunus Son of Clutor, Maelgwn in Welsh, commemorated in Latin and ogam, that early Celtic language brought here from Ireland in the fifth century. Bilingual inscriptions are rare, and this one has helped to provide the key to deciphering the ancient alphabet. It's tempting to assume that Clutor was the chieftain 'Clether' who granted Brynach the land for this church. If not, it's a strange coincidence. Embedded in the next window sill is another slab, about the same length, with a cross carved in relief on it. It is a strange, twisted cross suggestive of a human shape -a large triangular head with facial shaping and patterned knots at arms and pelvis. It seems very old and mysterious to me – Celtic in feeling but not in style – and though conscious that I shouldn't touch it, I cannot resist tracing the pattern with a fingertip. Who knows, perhaps that is what is was for – a sort of finger-maze, an aid to prayer or meditation.

On the lectern the Bible is open at a reading from Isaiah:

Mountains and hills will break into joyful cries before you and all the trees of the countryside clap their hands.

It suits my mood exactly.

In the porch is a plan of the graveyard and a plant list, meticulous in Welsh, Latin and English: 147 species, including 20 sorts of grass and 10 ferns. I have seen only snowdrops.

Outside is the famous Great Cross that legend says St David carried here on his shoulder. It towers in dappled shade. Photographs have not prepared me for its physicality. It stands before you like a presence, because of its size – tall as a small tree, thirteen feet – or, more likely, the complexity of what it is trying to say. Carved a thousand years ago in elaborate interlacing ribbons, each side has different centrifugal patterns – knotted braids and weaves and squares overlaid with circles. On the west side the letters *dns* are taken to stand for Dominus, and another inscription may mean Hallelujah. I think of Terry John's description of such stones: 'the petrified voices of our ancestors.' I feel no urge to reach out to these carvings, beautiful as they are. The head stares, owl-like but blind, across the graves. I would not be surprised by old tales that at night it walks.

'Many a pilgrimage ends at Nevern,' I've heard, and the number of graves does seem disproportionate to the size of the village. Past sunny walled plots of children's graves where birds sing and build, I pause at a surprisingly personal note on the headstone of 'Husband and Wf John and Ann Griffith, Deepwell, 1813 and 1818':

> Still we'll mourn
> For they to uf were dear
> And still ARE dear
> Tho' buried in the duft.

Down the dark avenue of massive yew trees, red as iron in some places – the second one drips blood – and out through the lych–gate I notice the mounting – block, like a solid bridge with six stone steps either side. Ladies and gentlemen could arrive at church with no loss of dignity. And no worries about who would take care of the horses during the service.

Time for a walk. So – misreading the map – I follow a track that I think will lead me to the Pilgrim's Cross but find myself doing a circuit through fields, blurting and sloshing through a blubber of watery mud by stiles where cattle seem to have gathered. After the gales, each hoofprint is a bowl of leaf and twig soup. In places, the mud is deeper than my wellingtons. This is where I need my pilgrim's staff. Before tractors and cattle fed outside, was the mud any less? But think of draught animals, untarred lanes axle-deep . . . no wonder the pilgrim season didn't start until the winter rains were over.

I am following a faint trail in the grass in search of what my map calls a 'cup-inscribed stone' when snipe startle me by rising almost from under my feet, four or five at a time twisting away in a low, zigzagging flight and turning like planes in old films to show their white underbellies. Watching them my eye is caught by a big sandstone disc, rearing up in the middle of the field. Can this be it, a waymarker on an ancient route? It's pitted and scratched, but I can see nothing that might be deliberate marks. A good vantage point with Carn Ingli on the left, it would have been a suitable place to point the way to the sea, and south to St Davids. As the vapour trails of three aircraft

heading out over Ireland and the Atlantic, straight and purposeful as arrows, are doing right now.

Just before the path veers back to the road there's a bobbing white scut: a rabbit bounces along slowly before disappearing into the hedge. Climbing the stile, I see what looks like a church – there's a bellcote – in a small copse a couple of fields away. In 1603, George Owen recorded eight pilgrims' chapels in this parish, even then mostly in ruins, presumably part of Henry VIII's 'reorganisation' of the Church and the ban on pilgrimages. Might this have been one of them?

St Andrew's, Bayvil – possibly once Norman French Beauville: it is a sheltered, south-facing, well-watered spot – is a tiny stone church ringed with hawthorns. Its *llan* is a tangle of bracken and blackberry, in places trampled down and dunged by horses which have found their way in. On the south side there seem to be the footings of a tiny building or a hermit's cell. It is very peaceful.

Inside is a surprise. I step into a box, brimming with light. White walls and panelled ceiling, cream-painted wood reflect and intensify the sunlight streaming through the high triple-arched windows (Gothic, I learn later.) There's a smell of warm paint and softening wood, but no damp. It's like early New England churches I have seen in films and *National Geographic*. A wooden altar rail is all that marks the sanctuary, and the space is dominated by a huge chapel-like pulpit –also panelled and painted – so tall the sounding-board above nearly touches the ceiling. It has a lectern and perches for three. There is only one memorial tablet. 'Thomas Lloyd of Cwmgloyne (1788) and Morris Williams (1840) who succeeded the above' might well have planted the woods I have just walked through, now a nature reserve.

Facing the pulpit are six box pews, like loose boxes in a stable except for the narrow benches, and in front of it is what must be a bier on a stand. So perhaps the occasional funeral still takes place here. There is what looks like a scatter of confetti on the three steps up to the pulpit: it is the tatters of Red Admiral wings.

For some reason one of Jung's dreams comes to mind: alone on a hiking trip in a hilly landscape he came across a small wayside chapel. The door was ajar and he went in, to find it bare- no altar, not even a crucifix – but in the centre a yogi in the lotus position, in deep meditation. Approaching, Jung saw that the face of the yogi was his own, and woke with the terrible conviction that his whole existence was only part of someone else's dream . . .

And R.S.'s voice :

no services now; the screen has nothing
to hide . . .

I keep my eyes
open and am not dazzled,
so delicately does the light enter
my soul from the serene presence
that waits for me till I come next.

The sun – *sun!* – streams in through clear windows and the wind moves shadows across the wooden floor; the only sound is birdsong. It is utterly peaceful and undisturbed, and I am glad to sit down. But more than that is a sense of wholeness. This isn't an old church – at least this building can't be more than a couple of hundred years old, the Nonconformist influence is so strong. (Later I am to read a description of it as 'A modest but evocative late Georgian structure'). It's clearly no longer in use – looked after by the Society of Friendless Churches, it's eight months since the last person signed the Visitors' Book, and yet there's serenity welling from somewhere. I have been reading the work of Waldo Williams, the visionary Welsh-language poet of this area. I remember his word 'balm', and lines from 'Adnabod' ('*Acknowledge*', in Tony Conran's translation):

Ti yw'r eiliad o olau	You are the moment of light
Sydd a'i naws yn cofleidio'r yrfa.	That embraces the way we pass.
Tyr yr Haul trwy'r cymylau –	The Sun breaks through the clouds –
Ti yw Ei baladr ar y borfa.	You're His radiance on the grass.

A little later, I come across the ruins of Nevern Castle. All that's left: grassy ramparts bright-flecked with celandines, a moat of brown leaves and bramble where the tower would have looked towards the glitter of the sea. *Mieri lle bu mawredd.*

Then, where the path follows the river down to Newport, in a glade of beech trees is the Pilgrim's Cross, a wayside shrine on the route from Holywell to St Davids. Three handspans high, the cross carved in relief on a wall of shaly rock is blurring under a patina of creamy lichen. I try kneeling on the ledge hacked out underneath, but it is too high and too shallow – it tips you backwards. More likely I should leave an offering. The small waterfall to the left would have made this place a natural refreshment stop in summer, its shade and the coolness of the rock – decorated with stonewort and ferns- most welcome. Moss has softened boulders into seats facing Brynach's hill of angels, and a few yards away rocky steps twisting up through the wood have been shaped into his footprints – I estimate size 9 – with a graffiti cross in the sole of the third.

It's almost 4 o'clock by the time I get back to the car, so I drive up Ffordd Bedd Morus to Carningli Common for a feel of the place and the buzzard's eye-view of the coastline. Twenty minutes' stumbling along pony tracks between low bilberry bushes, with dead heather witch-clawing at the ankles, is enough. The Preseli hills are already too dark to see the route over Foel Eryr, and I slide down into shadowy valleys following the Gwaun towards the sea.

SAINTS AND STONES
(Llanwnda, Llanstinan and Mathry)

Relying on finding vacancies out of season, I am lucky with the Ivybridge: it's warm and welcoming, they don't bat an eyelid at my trousers (mud over the knees) and even clean my shoes. A comfortable bed and an indulgent breakfast later, I'm up and over the hill marked on the map 'Stop and Call' to wild and windblasted heath where lanes tilt and narrow towards the sea. What few trees there are – hawthorn, sloe – all bend in the same direction, away from scouring southwesterlies. This headland is rich in prehistoric sites and I am

starting to see Significant Stones everywhere – there's a ring-cross marking the track to Cilau, where Joan Hague, a Bardsey friend, lives. From her garden we watch the ferry on its way to Rosslare, startlingly white against the grey water. She gives me coffee, a Saints and Stones teatowel and a book that is to save my bacon: *How to Study an Old Church*. A muddy track passes behind her tiny Pembrokeshire-pink cottage to Llanwnda Church – the way Goodwick-landed pilgrims would have walked.

Half a mile away, under the rocky cliffs of Carreg Wastad, is the site of the last invasion of the British Isles where in February 1797 four French ships dropped anchor and landed 1400 soldiers. Their back-up never arriving, for two days the French rampaged, getting drunk on a farmer's wedding supplies.

And in a scatter of white cottages and a huddle of farm sheds, asbestos roof lifting in the wind off the sea and a battered caravan hunching down in the scrub is St Gwyndaf's, a long, solid grey building, squat to defy the wind. Its leaning headstones are surrounded by walls the ivy is working busily to bring down, and blackbirds are noisy in alder thickets. Even the most neglected church goes on being a refuge, nowadays for wildlife: bats, swifts, swallows and martins, yews full of birds' nests and overgrown corners a haven for wrens, small mammals and insects.

Inside, it is so cold I can see my breath hang in the air and very still – almost resentful. This is a big church, with two aisles and chantry chapels, a high, vaulted roof of beams dark with age. (If you go, look for the tonsured face on the beam – I missed it.) An uninviting stone bench runs along the back wall and there's a 'squint' or peep-hole where people at the back – the poor? the sick? – could see the altar. There's a stale splendour about the eagle-headed lectern and the Bible under glass near the altar – a Parry Bible, already 175 years old when the French marauders stole the plate and set light to the church, tearing out – it is said – pages to use as kindling. I am told later that it was the Parish Record they used – and, good Catholic boys presumably, they'd carefully torn out only the unused pages from the back. There is also a huge key, 200 years old, which a note explains is displayed only as a symbol of an *unlocked* church.

There has been a church here since at least the eighth century, but the earliest fragments are disappointing lumps of sandstone pitted like thawing snowballs. I can make out the shape of a hand on one of them, but the carvings built into the outside walls are more convincing, especially the woman's face peering out from under a shawl; perhaps it is a monk's hood.

South of the church the ground falls away steeply, and the overgrown graves are very old, low footstones or thick bedhead markers. Against the wall once-imposing Victorian tombs dominate, ivy holding out its stiff little bouquets of black berries towards the names of important local families, the Mortimers and Williams, one of them Mary Anne:

An affectionate wife,
a tender and loving mother,
a hospitable and cheerful friend.

She died aged 36 in April 1868, and was buried with her third and fourth daughters – Mary Melena, 10 months old, and Cathlene Selena, 13 months in 1866. I can't help playing with dates, constructing a narrative: what carried off these three in three years? This was not a poor family. The great gamble of birth had been won; both babies had survived their first winter, and Mary Anne was healthy enough to conceive her fourth daughter before the third was weaned, for Cathlene Selena was born a matter of weeks after her sister's death. I wish I had more than a sketchy, Bronte-inspired idea of consumption. Perhaps it is the bleakness of the surroundings that brings that family to mind: the yew trees dripping now with rain, the stunted grass, the heavy elaborate tombs in their wrought-iron enclosures. There's a kind of allegory in the way the most imposing monuments have decayed soonest: marble stained and cracked, slate facing split and fallen, curlicued epitaphs unreadable, while many of the plainer headstones carry their names and dates into a third century.

I come away from a delightful lunch in Scleddau with the Easthams, Mike and Anne, with my head reeling with details of orthostats, mole-bones in neolithic middens, French cheeses, and churches I should visit.

Anne is evangelical about present-day pilgrimage. 'It takes people to explore the countryside, their heritage – places they wouldn't go to on their own.' Her Saints and Stones group got the first one going in August 1995 and there is a network of 32 churches open now, on three different routes. 'And it works! In 1994, here at Llanstinan we had no visitors. In 1997, two hundred people signed the Visitors' Book – and it's reckoned that only one in eight bother to sign. It brings a bit of money into the rural economy too.'

The Young People's Pilgrimage is the most enjoyable. 'Music all the way from Llanhywel to St Davids.' It's on Easter Monday this year, the summer ones still at the planning stage. She tells me about the last walk – lunch for seventy people at this little church, the route through St Nicholas, from Llanrhian to Llandeloy, 'Thirty-two of us and a dog', eight and a half miles in the pouring rain. Every time they try a new route they come across ancient footpaths on farmland and forestry closed or obstructed.

I would never have found St Justinian's without her for its village, Llanstinan, has disappeared. With the coming of the post road at the end of the eighteenth century – French prisoners from the 'invasion' were used in its construction – people moved and the settlement of Scleddau grew around the Gate pub. All that remains of the original village are the terraces of their gardens, with rambler roses in the hedges, the overgrown foundations of a two-room school and a tumble of stone by the stream named to Anne as a cottage called 'The Milking Stool.'

She leads me half a mile along a track older than Christianity (she has just told me how to recognise a Bronze Age bridge), now under a rash of notices about gates and dogs and Private Property. It's an all too-familiar story: Church Cottage has been sold at a price too high for locals, the land let to a sheep farmer from miles away and the new owners – London professionals seeking a rural retreat for occasional weekends, it seems – are set to 'improve' their investment, which may mean a certain lack of friendliness towards church visitors. Already there are coils of barbed wire and the hedges of the old village gardens have been slashed to the ground.

The churchyard is circular, the sign of an ancient *llan*, and probably of a site sacred long before. Seven springs are supposed to flow from beneath it. There are huge boulders in the enclosing wall, and a ring of ash trees thick with winter-resting buds. Anne tells me how in Brittany the ash is associated with the cult of Non: can the Welsh name, *onnen*, be coincidence?

The church is tucked under the hill, blending into the land. The only movement is in the sky: clouds rippling, their shadows moving steadily as flocks across the valley under the white sun's arch.

It is a pre-Conquest church: there is medieval masonry discernible on the west wall, and the bulge of the original hermit's cell, igloo-like, on the south.

The air inside is welcoming, warm after today's hours of sun, and smells faintly of dry grass and clean stone. I am surprised, in an unused church, to see flowers – it's only as I touch the petals that I realise, of course, they are artificial. The walls are whitewashed, and there is a thick low arch, like a cave, slightly askew, looking towards the sanctuary, but too large to be just a squint. Whatever its purpose the archway makes the church mysterious, a place to be explored.

Unusually there is a burial in the sanctuary, to the right of the altar – the most sacred place of all. Possibly even more surprising is that it is not a personage but a baby, and a diminutive rather than a formal name is used. Fanny Owen only lived from November 7th to January 9th – two months and two days- and was buried here in 1835.

I write in the Visitors' Book, my name and 'Aberdaron/Enlli' and flick through the pages crowded with signatures up to September last year.

Henry – a year older without you

A nine-year-old writes in August: 'The church is beautiful. I bet it's really sunny when the sun comes out.'

Even writing in this book feels like being part of history.

When Anne has gone home I come back to walk up to the Iron Age hillfort on the hill above and to go round the churchyard on my own. There's a different kind of response to places when you're alone, an energy that comes from solitude – more than a lack of distraction. It is easier to know what you feel. In this hour I am aware of soaking up the spirit of the place, a ripeness, as though people have been good and happy here. In Waldo's phrase, '*rhyw hen dangnefedd fel gweddi ddirgel*' ('some old peace like an ancient prayer').

★   ★   ★

I take the first turning up to Mathry in late afternoon of a vivid winter sunset. The silhouetted shapes of its buildings heaped on the hilltop like a fort or a Bunyan Promised City have beckoned me for miles. I pass a school, a farm – more mud escaping across the road – and then I seem to have reached the centre. There's the churchyard and staring across at it, a tall-windowed warehouse of a building, rather dilapidated, its vivid blue paint flaking so only the words General Stores are decipherable. The only movement is from a single mud-spattered sheepdog scratching in the road where I park by the Village Hall, a high old building that could have been a tithe barn. RS's *Village* comes to mind. You remember, 'scarcely a street, too few houses/to merit the title, just a way between/the one tavern and the one shop . . .' Even down to the dog . . . none of the hot sun evoked by that poem, but Mathry too looks out over the slow world below, a golden landscape of fertile fields that made this place the centre of trade and commerce in the Middle Ages. Have I missed the main part of the village? Has it rolled downhill to the main road, like the ancient settlement at Llanstinan?

The church with its exotic round belltower sits in the middle of a round green island where a village square might be. Two ash trees guard the gate. The grass is long, a few snowdrops struggling out. A splash of colour turns out to be two traffic cones tossed over the wall at least one summer ago, for they are well grown in. The large porch announces the name of the church in both languages: Eglwys y Saith Merthyr/Church of the Holy Martyrs, and immediately strikes a family atmosphere with a soppy picture of a Labrador and a ginger kitten ('*Love your enemies. Matthew 5.4*') and a no-nonsense boot scraper.

It's a big barn of a building, an open, well-lit space, arranged for practicality rather than mystery. Rows of chairs, as if for a school concert, occupy the middle of the room. By the door are several kitchen tables, wipe-clean melamine. The air feels used, and there is a slight smell of roast-chicken flavour crisps. Perhaps something has been happening in here earlier today? This end of the nave is a children's play area, with cheerful rugs, bright plastic chairs – toddler-sized – and table, coloured pencils and a shelf of picture books. *On the Farm* rubs shoulders with *My Very First Bible*, *Postman Pat* and a series of Action Rhyme stories that looks fun: *Come into the Ark with Noah*, *March Round the Walls with Joshua*, *Share out the Food with Jesus* . . . I read them all, and details of the Cawl Lenten Lunch, and an appeal for groceries for Bosnia. Next Tuesday evening there's a talk: The Rural Community Faces Many Problems.

The pulpit is pushed right back against the wall, and the altar table and sanctuary seem to retreat discreetly. On the lectern, a hymn sheet:

Summer suns are glowing
Over land and sea.
Happy light is flowing
Bountiful and free.

Tucked away at the side is a bookcase of paperbacks, for borrowing or swaps – PD James, Margaret Atwood, John Grisham, a row of Mills and Boon. I am surprised not to find more 'churchy' titles.

A tapestry in bright wool makes Mathry look a lot livelier than I've found it so far. I look for postcards – I'm becoming a church souvenir junkie (my version of the lead badges pilgrims used to collect), but there are none. Or informative leaflets.

What about the seven martyrs, or the witch story? However, I am quite pleased at the lack of compromise for tourists: this building, literally the centre of the village, is a church for local people, and for everyday rites.

I've read of ancient gravestones built into the south wall and as I'm pulling back the ivy I hear voices. Two girls in navy school uniform and a lanky boy of about 13 are coming up the hill in a businesslike way – tea, telly, homework. Or farm chores, a pony to see to before dark? I wonder how far they have to travel, and in view of the evidence of plenty of youngsters in the area, if the village school is still thriving. In the confidence of my new investigative role I stand on a stone to make my presence felt, lean over and call a cheerful greeting. (Having met a chilly reception in the shop when I asked for a pint of milk, I speak in Welsh.) Shock checks their stride for an instant. Their heads go up like cattle spotting someone in their field, and all three give me a blank stare. I sense teenage telepathic channels zipping to red alert: *Say nothing! Stranger, madwoman! Walk past, no eye contact, shields up!* Though I try again in apologetic English. 'I'm just having a look at your church. Would you mind telling me where you go to school? I just thought, there doesn't seem to be much going on in the village . . .' they sweep stiffly past, and only round the corner relieve themselves with a gurgle and helpless giggles. I glance round to see if my embarrassment has been witnessed – not a curtain twitches, no watcher in the shadows by the telephone box stifles a cough . . . What sort of village is this? At home, a stranger outside the tourist season is carefully observed, if not actually interrogated. It's news. Surely wandering around with my reporter's notepad at the ready is a badge of harmlessness?

My shadow's disappeared. Colour has drained from the fields below, the network of roads leading everywhere else. Which way down shall I take?

CIRCLING CLOSER TO SOMEWHERE
(Mesur-y-Dorth to Llanrhian)

The straight line never had much relevance to pilgrim routes, I'm sure: the chances of the road must always have been leading them into detours to shrines or other sacred places. The Latin *peregrinus* <u>means</u> wandering. Circling around or approaching a shrine in a sort of spiral was sometimes thought to intensify its power. So though I can see Carn Llidi, I decide not to make straight for St Davids today.

I start by finding the famous stone at Mesur-y-Dorth, where pilgrims from the north are supposed to have shared their last meal before reaching the shrine, although another story relates to David's decree restricting the size of loaves in time of famine. It is another ring cross, this time plump as a hot cross bun. From here I head north, beginning to tune in to the different energy of having sea on both sides. It's like Llŷn, that other long arm of Wales reaching towards Ireland, but softer, and more tended: we have more wire fences, usually flapping with witch-tatters of black plastic from silage bags. We have *cloddiau*, too – stone-faced earth banks, planted with gorse, hawthorn and blackthorn or rapidly colonised by honeysuckle, red campion, cow parsley and the white froth of scurvy-grass, with wild violets, primrose and harebells in their respective seasons. But they need skill in the making and maintenance, and you can bulldoze them out and stick up metres of wire fence in a day. Cheap, convenient – and yet the winter wind-shelter for cattle and walker alike, the deep green shade in summer, the wildlife highway is lost for good. Where will lizards bask? The burrowing wasp find shelter? Hopefully, they are all still here, in Pembrokeshire.

Abercastle is trimly kept, the quarrymen's cottages painted in smart postcard colours – pink, white, orange, yellow – roofed with silvery slates. This is working Pembrokeshire re-inventing itself as St Ives. Once a thriving little port, known for smugglers and shebeen, sloops carrying corn and butter (from the rich farmlands round Mathry) and bricks to Bristol, now it's literally a backwater, just a couple of boats – *Awel-y-Mor* and *Gwylan*, *Seabreeze* and *Seagull* – on trailers waiting for the season to start. On the side of a huge old granary a sign (in English only) announces Toilets, but despite a notice that says they will be open from mid-February and during school holidays (it is both), they are utterly impregnable.

The tide's out, exposing mud so dense and smooth it is like brown flesh. I love the way a skim of salty water reflects the sky, gleaming like ice so you feel you could slide from one side of the bay to the other. The sand is drying in creases, but where fresh water meets salt at the sea's edge there are hypnotic swirls and lagoons teeming with microscopic life:

As I watch
my brain is an estuary, shallow
dazzled with plankton, cells
at the tide's mercy, idling.

Matter watching itself.

(Anne Cluysenaar, 'Quarry'.)

From the sea, Carreg Samson must be dramatic against the skyline. It squats 'like a cauldron on three legs' as poet John Ormond puts it, the shaggy mushroom of its huge capstone bright yellow with lichen. The uprights are not much taller than me, but the out-of-proportion capstone gives this cromlech more raw power than Pentre Ifan. The massive boulder – sixteen feet long , nine wide – was heaved into place probably about 5,000 years ago as part of the central chamber of a polygonal passage grave. I have been told of dramatic effects on dowsing rods here. Even with the sun warm on my back and the sea glittering, I don't feel like staying long.

The cromlech field is shared with six well-grown Charolais cross bullocks hanging out morosely round a big bale of hay. From the state of the ground, they spend most of their day careering around and charging each other, seeing who can make the longest skid-marks. However, this morning, they only look across at me incuriously. They're used to tourists; there are three or four caravans over the hedge.

In the farmyard at Longhouse, there's a tractor I recognise as a John Deere because the bits that aren't covered in mud are bright green. Its bonnet cover is raised and a man is gazing in much as the cattle had looked at me, as though he wouldn't be surprised by anything. He's waiting for his brother-in-law, the mechanic of the family; needs to get it right in time for ploughing. But it's still too wet to get on the land at all. A Land Rover rackets up before I can ask how many of these big, level fields are down to corn nowadays, as when this was the grange for St Davids – the bread-basket of the peninsula in the Middle Ages. Good grain to the tomb's doorstep.

A footpath cuts across more soggy pasture and a couple of arable fields. It feels high and exposed up here; the sky looms, dwarfing me. I am happy to get back to the ups and downs and turns of the cliff path with its springy turf (I typed spongy, which was also appropriate in the dips), cowslip leaves, thrift, and short, prickly grass. Chough scream and tumble as I pause to eat the bacon sandwich saved from yesterday's breakfast. It tastes good: I must be hungry. I don't know how long I sit looking out to sea, breathing the warmth that rises from the busy earth.

Then down to the rockpools of Aberfelin and the tumbled heap of stones that was one of the two watermills here owned by the bishop of St Davids. It stopped working in the middle of the nineteenth century, but walking here one Sunday evening in 1918, William Crwys Williams (three times winner of the Crown at the National Eisteddfod), wrote what has become one of the most loved Welsh poems, that even I can recite:

Nid yw'r felin heno'n malu	The mill does not grind tonight
Yn Nhrefin ym min y mor.	At Trefin on the edge of the sea.
. . . Ond does yma neb yn malu	. . . But nobody grinds here,
Namyn amser swrth a'r hin	Except sullen time,
Wrthi'n chwalu ac yn malu,	Busy scattering and grinding,
Malu'r felin yn Nhrefin.	Grinding the mill at Trefin.

Lost in this translation is the repetitive sound, the emphasis on abandonment – *nid, neb, namyn-* and the strong flavour of smashing, destroying, in '*malu*.' Sometimes as piquant contrast, more often echo of loss, I stumble on evidence of 'change and decay' everywhere on this journey; how much keener it must have been with the shattering of families and traditions during the fourth year of the Great War when Crwys wrote his poem.

Back up the road to where I left the Renault is Trefin, another straggle of houses where it's hard to imagine the fairs and festivals, the courts and ceremonials of the past when the Bishop had a residence here.

Llanrhian Church has a solid stone wall all round it and a square belltower whose roof is strangely stepped. The effect is of twin pinnacles, an incongruous mix of the decorative and the defensive. An open bell-cote is more usual: the tower proves thirteenth century importance. Or the need for a look-out and stronghold (we are less than a mile from the sea here). Tower and church don't quite match, the nave seeming to crouch beside it and I find out later that though there has been a church here since the sixth century, the last of many rebuildings was in Victorian times.

Mossy stones line the path from the lych-gate. As I pass through, rooks lift from the few trees and float away like pieces of burnt paper. At the base of the north wall is another ancient cross, this one with a double circle, the outer only just traceable.

'To protect wildlife and the church, please ensure these gates are kept closed when the inner door is open.' The gates are what you would expect in a practical farming community, no-frills welded iron frame with wire mesh infill. In the porch, notices for whist drives and the Mother's Union meetings as well as the usual flower rota. A lecture on Organic Farming, and a website address: *healingtheland*.*org.uk* On Wednesdays, cups of tea are available. ('Only in summer' in pencil underneath.)

The inner door opens easily on to a spruce-green carpet and slight mustiness. The nave stretches away into shadow. I find a bank of light switches, conveniently placed and carefully labelled: Nave, Chancel, etc. I snap on Transept, and the effect is almost theatrical – warmth and colour, the sense (as in another RS empty-church poem) of a performance about to begin.

The impressive ten-sided font has one coat of arms – three ravens – the other nine panels are left plain. Was this an early play for sponsorship that never happened? But a row of thirty brand-new bright red hymn books is a hopeful sign that this church is well-attended today, not just carefully maintained.

A verse or two from Genesis seems appropriate:

And the Lord God took the man, and put him into the garden of Eden to dress it and to keep it . . .

On the way out I notice a polite note: 'Donations towards ongoing maintenance both inside and out will be most gratefully received.'

There's a small framed arrangement of dried pansies and ivy leaves round the words 'Thank you for your donation.' I have only small change to spare now, but make a silent promise to return.

The lower half of the graveyard – south, where the first graves would have been, to avoid the church's shadow falling across them – is abandoned to bramble and ivy. As I attempt a circuit, peering at lichen-stippled stones a cock pheasant rockets out, hiccuping alarm. Cattle milling about in a yard the other side of the wall start to bellow for another bale of the silage that fills the air with the smell of yeast and treacle.

The sky has faded to smoke grey. Over Manor Farm's twin silos it has the faintest mauve wash, with bands of pale sunset light. It's time for me to find somewhere to roost, too.

★   ★   ★

I am led to Caerhafod by the view and the standing stone in the field outside but the hostel accommodation in converted farm buildings is better than most guesthouses, and though Carolyn is rushing about between her children's tea and a newborn Welsh Cob foal, she makes time to give me a good welcome, even finding a potato for me to bake in the microwave.

A young couple are making tea in the big communal kitchen that looks out towards Carn Llidi. We have formal introductions. Iban Garcia Alcaraz and Lourdes Osborne (she is proud of her English grandfather) are from Cartagena in Spain. 'You know Alicante?' (what comes to mind is the tomato variety, but I nod; I can always look in the atlas later.) Both work in a big hospital in Reading – Iban (pronounced exactly like the Welsh Ifan) is an anaesthetist, Lourdes a nurse training in renal care and dialysis. There are good opportunities in the NHS for people like them, they tell me, many advertisements in Spanish newspapers. After finishing shifts at 9.30 the previous night they had set off on impulse, desperate for countryside, for horizons.

'We have to get out of the city, so many people, and we are – we are just like machines,' Lourdes says.' We just work, work, and then sleep. We know nobody. And to see the sea.'

Iban breaks in: 'Yes, but the best thing, in Wales, we find people are so friendly, they smile at us, say "Come in, have a cup of tea . . ." All my life, I have said hello to people in the street, smiled and said "Hello, how are you?" It is the way we are . . . but here, in England, in Reading, if you look at strangers or if you speak, you see them thinking "Crazy man, what does he want?"'

I decide not to tell them of my encounter in Mathry.

Last night they spent in a tent in the dunes behind Whitesands Bay, arriving at half past one in the morning. It was too cold to sleep – 'I was crying, "Please, Iban, please get in my sleeping bag with me, there is plenty of room, please keep me warm"'– so in the end they walked by the sea for hours looking at the amazing stars. When I tell them that they may have been on the site of David's original church, where the angel appeared to tell him to build in the valley, Lourdes' eyes grow huge. 'Then I am very pleased we will sleep here tonight, in case of ghosts.'

The Loss and Jubilation of the Cliffs
(Porthgain to Porthclais)

Sunday morning quiet, broken only by guillemots' gurgling low down on the rocks. The sea gleams like polished steel, but there's a fringe of white swell round the slabs fallen from the dark shale cliffs, and its slosh and boom in the coves has accompanied me round Trwyn Elen. There's a change of weather in the offing.

A last glance at Strumble lighthouse flashing bright against the grey, then I come over the hill past the lime-washed waymark that once guided ships in to the little hidden harbour of Porthgain. In here, almost enclosed, the sea hardly moves against the jetty. The ruins of the pilot house on the headland could be a Crusader castle and the bleak walls of the old kilns with their high slit windows a crumbling fortress. The brick is the exact shade of the dry bracken around and above them.

Parked beside the vast old engine shed ('Eat in/Takeaway, Homemade Soups') there's a dusty Mazda pick-up full of weldmesh lobster pots and a newish Transit – white, what else? – with a load of nets in blue plastic bins. No tang of bait though, – as a lobster fisherman's wife I'm attuned to that – so the fishing season hasn't started yet. Five or six houses perch on the hillside above a grassy square where there's a scamper of children and two big dogs. A chocolate Labrador lumbers over to investigate me, his tail swinging as though he's a wind-up toy.

Outside the Sloop Inn a neatly-chalked board offers 'Breakfast, 9.30–11.30: Croissants with Butter and Hot Chocolate, Bacon Sandwich or Full Pembrokeshire Fry-Up'. Underneath someone has added, in capital letters: *CWRW!* Despite the coffee and cheese roll in my rucksack, I am seriously tempted, though not by the beer. Not only the anticipation of fresh-roast coffee (or should I have the hot chocolate? Both?) but the idea of sitting here for a while, savouring today's quiet among reminders of the busyness of a hundred years ago, when the Boer Wars and then the rise of the motor car increased demand for road-stone. Where only the fishing-boats *Carolina* and *Mary Lou* are moored, there were ten at a time waiting to be loaded – ketches, smacks, schooners, queueing to get in. Three hundred men worked here; there were three steam locomotives, traction engines, a stone crusher rumbling all day. The air would have been thick with dust.

CLIFFS KILL. KEEP TO THE PATH is the message that follows me round from Porth Mawr (Whitesands Bay) to St Justinian's. I want to look out from where Patrick may have sailed to Ireland, and maybe – as saints and pilgrims must have done for centuries – glimpse gannets diving in Ramsey Sound.

The sea looks empty once I have left the mad windsurfers behind. But invisible corridors in the sky are full of traffic and voices: the afternoon is punctuated by contrails, sharp, white commas, heading west urgent as sperm, pointing downward towards Ireland or up and out to New York, Boston, Chicago.

I am vaguely guilty to be enjoying myself. Early Celtic Christians, especially Irish monks, don't seem to have regarded delight in nature as sinful but in Paul or Augustine's version, all pleasure of the senses is a lure for the soul. And wasn't a degree of hardship necessary for a satisfying pilgrimage?

I haven't sat in a church today, but I have felt what Catherine Fisher talks about in 'Hikers':

the rhythm of striding
releasing the mind like meditation;
the rosary of the road.
Nothing, after hours, but sky
a snatch of conversation,
a poem's line
like a mantra on hills and fells,

the trudging from somewhere to nowhere.

And what about St David's last instruction, on his deathbed: 'Be joyful'.

At Porthclais the river is galloping to the sea under a little stone bridge. I stand and look out over the long narrow inlet that has been such a busy place. The tide is in, but there are no boats (despite the guidebook's claim that this ancient harbour is 'now a pretty home of small pleasure craft') and no sound except the freshwater ripples and distantly, someone working with a spade. A lone cyclist hisses by with not a look to either side, intent on keeping his speed up the next hill.

It's an ancient harbour: it was here that the Twrch Trwyth, the Great Boar of the Mabinogion, came ashore, chased from Ireland by Arthur. David was baptised just up the hill in a well that must be now overgrown, for that whole side is a tangle of bramble even in this season. This was the port for the growing settlement at St Davids, uncountable cargoes of timber from Ireland, purple sandstone in cartloads from ships beached in the creek. The original breakwater was early medieval – from the time Gruffudd ap Cynan, father of Owain Gwynedd, landed from exile in Ireland and marched north to fight the Normans and seize his kingdom – but it has been restored twice since 1722. The old kilns either side of the quay were in full use until about a hundred years ago, burning limestone. It might have been brought here first to be used as mortar in the building of St Davids, but lime has been used to improve the land locally since Tudor times: 'It destroyeth the furze, fern, heath and other like shrubs growing on the land and bringeth forth a fine and sweet grass,' George Owen explained.

I wander over to what looks like a timber garden shed. WARNING – 24 HOUR CTV SYSTEM OPERATING. So even in this quiet place there is vandalism or theft. A list of legal fish sizes is displayed and an explanation of V-notching – a voluntary scheme to try to maintain lobster stocks by returning marked 'berried hens' (females carrying eggs) to the sea. A fluorescent yellow notice warns not to go too close to seal pups, and there's a yellowing newsprint cutting from what's claimed to be an Irish paper: 'WANTED, a good woman who can clean and cook fish and who owns a good fishing boat and motor. Please send photo of boat and motor.' Fishing humour.

The regular, repeated sound of a spade on dry earth has become part of the landscape by now. On a steep slope above the lay-by where a fishing boat called *C'est La Vie* is pulled up, a tall man has been digging vigorously ever since I walked down the hill. There's something about the angle of his head that tells me he's been keeping an eye on me, so I call out some comment on the dry weather, and the difficulty of his task. 'And I'm well into my eighties, you know,' he says, raising the spade higher as if to show the earth that he's still its master. 'I'll be eighty-five next.' I ask about the fishermen's shed, and he puts down his spade to come and tell me. He has a strong, lean frame, a spare, intelligent face and a sailor's eyes – blue but hazy with distant perspectives, with what has been left behind. He had given the land to the local fishermen when they needed somewhere, and they'd wanted to put his name on it. 'I told them, you put my name on it, you're not havin' it – I never wanted glory, never did anything for the glory of it. So – you see that sign?' I had not noticed the simple wooden board with the name *Patshyn Osi* (Osi's patch). 'For Oswald, my brother . . .'

He turns back to look up at the steep slope. 'I had this after my father. We had the farm, see –' he waves an arm towards Trefeiddan. His father made the journey here by boat from Dinas Island. There were four children, 'my older sister, she stayed on the farm, she was a good girl – in a Home now – and my other sister was in the Post Office in St Davids for years. And myself and Osi.' The farm was sold years ago, and he's supposed to be retired, but something keeps telling him to go out and work. 'I've always had energy, all my life.' He has ripped all the ivy off this ruined cottage, and worked for months to expose the good dark soil – covered in bracken and bramble and so thick with weed roots, he's had to dig it twice – to help the couple who want to buy the place and perhaps rebuild here. He feels he is putting something back. 'I've had a good life. I've been lucky.'

He looks at me quite sternly. 'If I weep, say nothing.' I wait and listen. 'He was always on at me to stay home and help my father. I'll go, he said. So off he went, was in Burma four and a half years. When he got home – well, he didn't last long, poor Osi. And he couldn't talk to us about it, never.'

He turns back to his digging, his mind full of presences from the past. 'I am proud,' he says, emphatically. It is a declaration that seems to surprise him, 'Proud of my family, all of them – good people, hardworking . . .'

The sun has disappeared over the hill by now and my hands are cold in the sharp breeze. We both shiver. 'Well – better get a bit more done before dark. It's been nice meeting you – you know, years ago I wouldn't bother with anybody. Too shy I suppose. Now, I like to have a word, to meet people from somewhere else.'

'I don't regret my life, I've enjoyed it.' It is a valediction. There is such dignity and acceptance in it, now it is I who turn away to hide my eyes.

There's a smell of clean air and earth. The wind has got up – the shirts and trousers hung out to dry outside the cottage on the hill have turned playful. I feel as though I can't store any more – the day has been rich – so I sit at a wooden picnic table by the water to scribble a few notes.

A robin hops up onto my foot and tilts his bright eye up towards my face. Such trust, or desperation; such vulnerability.

Bright in memory, the robin's eye and the turned earth drying reddish under the wind, the solitary man stubbornly digging, while the western sky flushes with rose and geranium, the promise of frost.

THE CITY IN THE VALLEY
(St Davids and the Cathedral)

The Blue Guide to Wales introduces St Davids with uncharacteristic realism: 'Because of its cathedral officially a city, in practice little more than a village straggling across an almost treeless and often either misty or wind-swept plateau above the boggy river Alun.' This is how I see it first, approaching from the sea up Glyn Rhosyn, the marshy valley and through Lower Moor. Even in ruins though the sheer size of the Bishop's Palace can't fail to impress and the dull purple stones of the Cathedral's west face have a foxglove gleam in the day's last sun.

I'm cold and in need of a meal; there should be plenty of places to choose from, but it's Sunday early in the year so it's dark by the time I'm settled in a small hotel at the top of Nun St.

I walk down the street to find a phone box – true to form, there is 'no service' on the mobile from my room – and a meal. Opposite the traffic island with the cross, where four boys are kicking a football across the road with cries of 'Score!' and 'Yes!', there is a Bistro. It's £2.95 for a glass of red wine and £6.90 for a plate of vegetables and rice, but there are real chrysanthemums, coloured candles in mock stained-glass holders, and rough-cast stone walls. There are only three other customers, a well cared-for American couple and a Japanese man a decade or two younger. They are deep in conversation as I am shown to a table opposite them. 'I was reminded how Jesus must have felt when he entered Jerusalem,' declares the young man. My food arrives – with complimentary poppadums – and when I next tune in, they are imagining Christ overturning the stalls in the Cathedral Gift Shop. 'Twenty-two appeals for money!' They turn to include me; it's something of a disappointment that I haven't yet witnessed the cause of their agitation. Have I heard that someone said the present Dean is more interested in buttresses than angels? They are especially indignant about a leaflet addressed to 'Our friends from the United States', and amazed that they had been the only celebrants at Evening Prayers. 'It kinda struck me as funny, that big bell tolling and the only thing responding was the birds – they were all flocking around, but no *people*.' 'And they want us to give money for more bells!'

Nos Duw ar Dyddewi (to misquote Waldo slightly). There is still a distant glow, not so much a light as a pulse, below a horizon that is the darkest of blues.

★   ★   ★

The landlady bustles in from frying eggs and mushrooms to tell me about the concerts in June. There's a combination of excitement and dread about the coming Eisteddfod: 'Everbody I know's fully booked already, I had the BBC on the phone yesterday —'

A well-built, bearded man comes down and orders breakfast 'as full as you can make it' in a New York accent. Dan Salt has come back to the site of a childhood holiday. He remembers the thrill of cooking sausages on the beach — and of being with the Queen for morning service in the cathedral. He calculates: it must have been 1955, summer. The Royal Yacht *Britannia* came right into Solva, there was great excitement, processions of schoolchildren.

His wife dead seven years, his children grown, he has taken early retirement from an airline 'to make the most of the rest of it, have a few jaunts.' In the next month he has trips booked to Seattle, Singapore and Sidney, but right now he's going to take it easy and learn all he can about the history of this important little place.

I browse the town for what's on offer locally. Showing tonight — *Serendipity*, 'a spine-chillingly romantic film starring John Cusack and Kate Beckinsale'. There's a lecture by Terry John on the Coastal Trade of North Pembrokeshire next week and the first of a series of Gardening Masterclasses. 'The Healing Garden', 'Springtime Propagation', 'Adventures with Colour': they all take my fancy. The Cathedral Women's Fellowship are hosting the Cleddau Dancers at a light buffet (with wine) at Ysgol Bro Dewi but Broadside Ballads and Seashanties at Porthgain are cancelled. Monday's shore-search at Manorbier sounds good.

I stand for ages at an exhibition of wildlife photographs, transfixed by close-ups: a horned alien, heraldic gold, is the Ramshorn Snail, last recorded in Wales in 1927; mussels like pearls and the wings of a Prussian Blue Southern Damselfly, each a net for light.

Having expected to spend a lot of time in the Cathedral, I am almost putting it off, exploring the town and the magnificent ruins of the Bishop's Palace first. But it turns out not to be journey's end.

Inside, it is even more imposing. I lose my bearings; used as I am to simple cross-shaped churches, I don't know where to go, find it hard to find a focus. It is a high-ceilinged hall, brisk with business-like activity, two people approaching with guidebooks, tourists milling about between points of interest, a little crowd by the bookshop, the occasional black-robed cleric on his passage from one door marked Private to another. I find myself staring at a display of souvenirs.

There is too much to take in – grand arcades, intricately carved ceiling, delicately fretted arches: I am just a sightseer. The way the organ dominates, shining above the nave as though it is being deified; the dignity of the rounded Norman arches; flowers perfectly matched and arranged on stands like a florist shop. I can't get over the contrast between the frugality of the saints – Dewi ddyfrwr and Stinan who sought an even harder life on Ramsey – and extravagant architecture, the lavishness all about me. And – though who am I to even think this? – in the whole place, with all its pulpits and altars and side chapels, there is no-one praying or sitting in contemplation.

I like the statue of David with a forked beard and shepherd-like crozier, and the icon from Crete showing Elijah being fed by the ravens, but find sickening the magnificence of Gower's tomb and his Bishop's Chair. That Oxford man who had walls built round the cathedral to keep the town out.

'If you have come to St Davids simply as a visitor, we encourage you to reconsider your life, your future and your faith. Cathedral clergy and staff are always willing to give help and advice.' But here's a group bustling past, (how can their feet be so noiseless even when they're hurrying – is special footwear prescribed?) I could be having a conversion right here *now* and they are too busy to notice – there's a meeting in the library (probably about fund-raising). The Cloisters Project needs £2.4 million. 'Quite a project,' someone reading the display board says, with a raised eyebrow, and moves away.

I pause at the tomb of the unknown priest, reputed to be Giraldus Cambrensis, d. 1223. Rector of St Gwyndaf's at Llanwnda before he came here and failed to become Bishop. Next is the Lord Rhys, 1107, very stern and cold. He gave land outside the city for the use of pilgrims. I'd say one for him. The floor is rising quite noticeably now. Does it get holier the further east you go?

Here's a glass case displaying the conifer-green cope worn by Bishop Jenkinson at Queen Victoria's coronation in 1838. I am sorry for his daughter Lady Maidstone having her hook nose immortalised in marble. She lies grandly outside the Lady Chapel which is screened off. I don't know whether I am allowed to try to go in, or not. Is it only for special days or services? I am drawn away by a kindly human face in relief on the wall – David Howell, A Good Man And Kin Of the Holy Ghost. He was vicar of Pwllheli in 1861: I feel an absurd tug of relevance.

There's a stillness in the light of St Thomas's Chapel. It's a human-sized space, and empty. I go in. An unadorned altar, a grey stone washbowl that looks very old – a piscina it's called. I have learned (from Joan's book) that they were to drain away into the earth any of the wine and water used in the Mass, to save it from profanation. There are chairs – the sort that creak through school assemblies – but for the first time I feel drawn to kneel. There is Thomas a Becket splendid in scarlet in the stained glass window. I think of the lice moving in the hair shirt they discovered under his robes after he was murdered.

My eyes are moving over the jewel-like colours, not thinking of anything in particular, just relaxing into being there, when the words at the bottom swim into focus: 'Remember Ernest Evans, Friend and Benefactor 1876-1957'. Ernest Evans is my husband's name; only half an hour ago I was thinking of talking to him. For a moment the potential for a Special Significance trembles in the air – then there's a disturbance behind me, two clerics sweep in, their swish of robes startling me. They are having a disagreement, about what somebody said. My mood is shattered. I can't believe it. Of all people! Should I point to the notice that says: 'St Thomas Becket's pilgrim chapel reserved for quiet prayer and meditation'?

They go. Closing my eyes, I lean my head on the altar rail to try and recapture the freefall of thought. I'd imagined this place as a fountainhead of spiritual energy. Instead it seems diverted back into itself. It feels purposeful, a workplace intent on itself like a college or a set of offices, nothing to do with me.

There have been voices, comings and goings, somewhere upstairs, and now there is a sudden screech, almost a scream from the organ – piercingly loud – and then thunder-rumblings so low their vibration hurts my ears. It sounds like a kid playing about, then steadies into a sombre tune; there must be a practice. I have had enough anyway.

Stamped at the top of every page of the Visitors' Book is 'Please put a donation in one of the boxes.' Three hundred thousand visitors a year. Perhaps buttresses are as important as angels. Angels can look after themselves.

LIGHTING A CANDLE
(Caerfai to St Non's)

I sit on the bench overlooking the beach at Caerfai to try to sketch the shapes: long grey fingers of land reaching out across St Bride's Bay – Midland Island, Skomer and a smudge that could be Grassholm where the gannets breed. Archipelagoes of cloud, the blackness of tumbled boulders against the translucent green sea. I have a double page of wide charcoal sweeps – it's the foreground that causes me trouble, always, what to select from the wealth of detail, how to keep the rest in focus – when I am disturbed.

A jackdaw flaps down clumsily to perch on the next bench, close enough for me to see his eyes are bright blue. His throat and nape are dark: a juvenile, an Artful Dodger trying his luck. He lifts his head feathers like a crest, looks at me with turned head and clucks interrogatively. This is a picnic spot, ok? Wouldn't I like to snack on a little something? Realising that a more intimate approach is needed (the equivalent of a car salesman's hand on the arm) he skips down and hops closer with an extraordinary range of soothing churrs – there's no-one else about, it will be just between us, no big deal – ending with emphatic nodding and a rapid series of clicks. *Poh-poh-poh-poh*.

I have a couple of Braeburn apples and a square of Pilgrim's Choice Vintage Cheddar, its black plastic wrap stamped repeatedly 'Handmade on the Farm'. Apparently, 'This cheese has a distinctive bite and is best complemented with strong red wine.' The jackdaw is too polite to mind taking it straight, though I get the impression it's not quite what he's used to in the few minutes before the rest of the gang screech in and drive him off. Embarrassed that I have broken the tranquillity of the place – and realising the breeze is chill on my back – I take the top path round the cliff.

On the point, the sea is white-flecked and ripples with conflicting currents. There's a surprising amount of heather, sharp, bleached stalks lining the path. Beyond is a thicket of bramble, blackthorn and gorse grown leggy like poorly-designed trees.

It is much warmer in St Non's Bay. Each wave breaks on the beach below with no more than a gentle hush and stonechats are busy in the bushes. For the first time this year I catch the scented tobacco smell of sunwarmed gorse. But then I am taken aback by the ugly grey house that dominates the bay. Its two rows of double-glazed windows stare uncompromisingly out to sea, give nothing away. This must be the Retreat Centre I've read about; there was an advert for a Sacred Dance Weekend in May ('To experience movement as meditation and worship, to be more fully in our bodies, more fully ourselves'). There are three Catholic nuns in residence who are always ready to lend a listening ear. I suppose it's all right looking out.

The ruins of what was the 'Chief Principal' of pilgrimage chapels here in the Middle Ages are in the next field, fenced round. This is where Non is supposed to have given birth to David in a thunderstorm (stones at various sites are said to be marked with her straining fingerprints). There was a stone circle here even then; it has probably been a holy site for four thousand years. The sun is warm on my shoulders as I push open the gate and cross the uneven pasture, noticing the verdigris shine of long-dried cowpats, as though they are turning into metal.

I feel silly, standing in the middle of a field gazing at four piles of stone. I try to look as though I know what I am doing, as though I remember all that Anne told me about identifying medieval masonry and the remains of Bronze Age circles. There's the gape of a chimney; the building was used as a dwelling after the Reformation. Facing north to south suggests foundations from a very early Christian period. In one corner stands my last cross-marked stone (from the ninth century or before), once built into the wall. The inscription is simple and perfectly-proportioned, so clear it could have been carved last year. I'm glad no-one has put it in a museum, that it is left to weather gracefully out here overlooking the sea and the islands.

The well — whose spring gushed forth gladly at the birth of the saint, of course — is clear to its sandy bottom where layers of coins

catch the light, some shiny, new-minted, many greened over. A stone hood or cowl arches over it, a baby's bonnet with a frill of whitewashed stones. It's a healing well, especially useful for eye problems. Babies and rheumaticky limbs were dipped in it – there are steps and sitting ledges just submerged. It is very full, and I am observing how the overflow runs down in a scattering twinkle, becomes a steady stream and changes tone – sinking a few octaves to a more serious tune – when two young women with cropped hair clatter down the paved path.

They've got a Ducati Monster (I have to be told it's a motor-bike, very powerful) parked at the top of the hill, but they've been walking all day, right round the headland to see Coetan Arthur and the tumbled stone parapets on Carn Llidi. It's wild, windswept heathland up there, they tell me, a world away from this gentle, gorse-scented air – really feminine, womb-like, this bay.

Ruby does the talking. Her friend is from Dusseldorf, and has taken the name Megan ('The Welsh thing is really big in Germany'). They are both enthusiastic believers in 'the Mother, all that'. We've had thousands of years of patriarchy and a father god so it's hard to remember a time when the earth was sacred, but we're getting back to it, not only women, lots of men too, now it's threatened and we're beginning to believe it. 'Whatever you feel in these ancient sacred sites, Christian or something older, circles and rituals, they're nourishing places – have you been to Lindisfarne, Skellig Michael, Iona? I can give you the name of a really good B&B . . .' They talk about telepathy, phases of the moon and a network of light across the world, letting their arms trail languidly through the water, then, cupping their hands, each in turn rinsing their faces and sipping from their palms. 'We think of what we need to let go,' prompts Ruby as they scoop up another handful of water and turn to throw it away, Megan scattering it over the open flowers of a gorse bush, drop by drop.

They have enthused about the Catholic chapel at the retreat centre – 'the most westerly in Wales!' It's a replica of St Non's, built of stones from old churches. So I walk back to the small modern building with a wooden bench along the wall, seat well polished on the sunset-watching side.

The door is open. Smaller than Bayvil, and full of colour, as medieval churches were. Red and yellow chrysanthemums on the altar, daffodils on the windowsill – and so much stained glass. It's twentieth-century of course but to my ignorant eye the images are as crafted as those in the cathedral, and more moving because they're simpler. St David in sunset light looks older, tired even; Brynach is still kindly, the cuckoo on his shoulder here. And women are well represented: Winifred is a golden-haired princess, all green and gold, with a sword and a leek, St Bride a blue-robed nun blessing the fishes.

Twice my height, the statue of Our Lady has a long aristocratic nose and a supercilious, Head Prefect expression, but the toenails and folds of her cloak are beautiful. She drapes a discreet finely-carved stone nappy over The Divine Child who is resting one plumply-dimpled foot on what looks like a football – except that it's covered in stars. Creation itself.

There's a white heart-shaped stone cemented into the centre of the altar, from the excavations of St Patrick's chapel on Whitesands Bay in the 1930s. On the communion table are prayers and poems, some handwritten. 'Finally on my way to yes' is one, and a page of gnomic statements about facing the empty loom. 'The loom without is the loom within.' Whether I understand them or not, I read them all aloud as has become my practice. Right at the end, there's a single line in calligraphy on a card:

God grows everywhere, like grass

I recognise it with delight, and the name below – it's a quote from Kelly Cherry, a poet from Wisconsin I met on Bardsey seven or eight years ago. She was staying in Hendy, the house next to the Abbey ruins. I wonder what's happened to her; whether she was here, where else her writing has taken her.

St Non Pray for Us. 'Petitions are placed before the altar during our times of prayer.' Folded slips of paper are provided printed in blue, with 'May God hold you in the palm' of his hand on the back. You write your petition and leave it in a wicker basket. It's brimming with messages. Does anyone read them? Why is it better to write them and have them put on the altar during prayers than to say them yourself in this place?

What is prayer anyway, does it need to be voiced? In his poem 'Morning-Watch' the Metaphysical Henry King said it was just 'the World in tune'.

Four candles are burning steadily beside a framed verse:

May this holy light
quiet the voices that confuse my judgement
and cloud my heart's true vision
that I may step forward with light
and courage in my heart.

There's a throw-away gas lighter for the candles. They're practical, these people. I light a fifth one. Its flame burns strongly, straight up. Is that significant? Is there a tradition that it means purity of heart, or have I just made it up? The other candles are well burnt down, one almost going out, guttering. I put my pound coin in and take another candle, pressing it gently into the soft wax, keeping the light going. Then I sit on the nearest chair and let my eyes rest on its small circle of gold.

My mind floats, thinking of the scent of gorse, of sun on grass, of Kelly's book *Natural Theology* that I'll take down from the shelf when I get home: the passionate, pagan Christianity in her poems. I have been surprised, these last few days, how much poetry has come back to me, other people's words welling up to fill the gaps in my experience. I try to remember if it was Pascal who had the wager with himself about believing in God, that he stood to lose nothing if he was wrong, but he'd be a damned fool if he wasn't.

I remember the churches I have been in, their different atmospheres. Cluttered, lived-in Mathry. Bayvil, deliberately plain and Quakerish. St Brynach's taking me under its wing. Llanrhian of the rooks, and the island tranquillity of Llanstinan. Slightly grim St Gwyndaf's at Llanwnda, looking back not forward. And this – St Non's new place – gentle, generous towards our modern pick 'n' mix search for meaning. What sadness there is here is all abstract; there are no graves. No memorials, just the moment.

There are other thoughts too, the words for them not grasped yet, gleaming just out of reach, like pennies in water.

I pick up two of the prayer petitions. 'To remember Robin Reeves,' I write, 'for whom I made this journey.' On the second I put, more hesitantly: 'for H. that she gets well and happy at Llanrhystud'.

I don't shrug on the way out. In fact, I feel more like crossing my fingers.

★   ★   ★

The ploughing is under way. Two tractors move steadily up the field, unrolling corduroy furrows to the skyline. A great swoop of gulls soar and turn and shine, with crows black as clerics bustling below. All the ash trees are haloed, their branches combed by the wind and the low angled sunlight catches on bracken stalks, picks out detail in the hedges: the plumping cushions of scurvy-grass, almost lime-green, celandines glittery as foil.

A yellow sky to end the day. It will get dark quicker tonight, light already thickening around the rooky wood by the Warpool Court Hotel. There's a change in the weather, a swirl of cloud sweeping in from the west again. And quite suddenly, time snaps into place around me. Tomorrow there's the WEA class and the painting group in Tremadog. It would be nice to be there. I'm not booked anywhere, nobody is expecting me. I am free to go home. In four and a half hours, or five, I could be walking in.

I start the search for a phone box that works. Phone cards only.

'We only do Pay-As-You-Go for mobiles now. Try the Post Office.'

'Don't seem to have any, sorry.'

Oh well. I'll just set off and maybe surprise them.

I walk back over Pont Cerwyn Dewi to the car parked opposite the Palace. The other vehicles have all gone, coachloads whisked off on the next stage of their tour, the early-retireds already planning which garden or stately home is next, students and possibly writers scuttled back to guest-house rooms to scribble notes by 40-watt bedside lamps. The trees are beginning to stir to the coming storm. In twos and threes teenagers are drifting down the hill towards the ruins.

Glancing left as I turn on to the A487, the middle way out of St Davids, I see a swarm of late afternoon flights heading out towards Ireland, at that altitude catching the sun already below our horizon. I head north from a sky still full of falling light.

NOTES ON CONTRIBUTORS

DAVID W. JAMES (1910-2002) A native of Cilgerran, he was educated at Cardigan Grammar School and University College of Wales Aberystwyth where he obtained his M.A. in 1936 with a thesis on James Joyce. He began his teaching career at Milford Central School and, after War Service, moved to Fishguard County School where he became Head of English. He was Headmaster of Ysgol Dewi Sant, St. Davids, from 1959 to 1974. In 1981 he published *St Davids and Dewisland* and, in 1995, *Twice to St. Davids*. He contributed to numerous journals including *New Welsh Review*.

JIM PERRIN is a prose stylist who has a head for heights to match his sense of a sentence. He is a regular contributor to *The Great Outdoors*, *Climber* and *The Daily Telegraph* and has written many books about landscape and travel, including *Visions of Snowdonia*, *Spirits of Place* and *River Map* in which he followed the Dee in the company of photographer John Beatty. His biography of John Menlove Edwards won the Boardman Tasker award in 1995 and recent journeys – from the High Arctic to Hungary – are chronicled in the volume *Travels With The Flea*.

ROBERT MINHINNICK was born in 1952 in Neath (the maternity hospital in Maesteg being full). He is a poet and essayist, his most recent collections being *Selected Poems* (1999) and *After the Hurricane* (2002) both from Carcanet. He has been awarded the Cholmondeley Prize, plus the Forward Prize for 'best individual poem' in 1999. In 1993 his essay collection, *Watching the Fire Eater*, was 'Book of the Year' in Wales. In 2003 Carcanet will publish his translations of contemporary Welsh-language poets. He lives in Porthcawl where he edits the international quarterly magazine *Poetry Wales* from an attic from which he can see both Exmoor and the Bridgend valleys.

PATRICK DOBBS left school at seventeen to work on an Exmoor farm. Later, he studied agriculture at Wye College, London University, then led a nomadic life working in Canada and South America, before settling on a small farm in Llanddeusant where he has remained ever since. Once heavily involved in agricultural journalism and deeply committed to his farm, he now farms for fun and only writes for his own enjoyment. His two children have wisely distanced themselves as far as possible from both agriculture and Wales. His prose diary appears in *A Year in a Small Country* (Gomer, 1999) and his poems are often combined with performance at cultural events and readings in south Wales.

JON GOWER is the arts and media correspondent for BBC Wales. He has written *An Island called Smith* about a doomed community in Chesapeake Bay and a collection of short stories called *Big Fish*. He has also edited various volumes including *Homeland* and *A Year in a Small Country*. He is currently working on the history of his home village, Pwll.

OSI RHYS OSMOND is an artist and lecturer based in Llansteffan, Carmarthenshire. A regular contributor to magazines such as *Planet* and *New Welsh Review*, writing about subjects as varied as Welsh bus companies, peasant food, cultural amnesia and the language of the deaf, Osi has travelled widely, as his exhibitions about the Holy Land and the Sudan attest.

CHRISTINE EVANS lives near Aberdaron on the Llŷn peninsula, spending the summer months of every year on Ynys Enlli, Bardsey Island. Her publications include several volumes of poetry, beginning with *Looking Inland* (Poetry Wales Press, 1983) and, the most recent, *Island of Dark Horses* (Seren, 1999). Her prose appears in *A Year in a Small Country* (Gomer, 1999), in Gwasg Gregynog's series 'Places: Y Man a'r Lle' – *Uwchmynydd* (1998), and in several publications about Enlli. During her years as an English teacher, she edited two anthologies for young people: *The Blue Man & other stories from Wales* (Pont, 1995) and *Old Enough & other stories* (Pont, 1997) and wrote *Approaches to the study of Autobiography from Wales* (WJEC, 1998).

PAUL ADRIAN DAVIES was born in Cardiff and now lives on the Lower East Side of New York City. He has photographed this area of the city over a period of many years; his recent work includes 'A Neighbourhood Responds' which documented the community response to the events of September 11th 2001. Other projects include a series of images of signs, graffiti and murals from North America, Central America, Europe and South East Asia and 'Public Solitude' a study of the feelings of solitude experienced by people living in urban areas. He is currently photographing the changing character of the Barri Gotic and El Raval *barrios* of central Barcelona. He was the only pilgrim to walk the whole route, arriving at journey's end on St. Davids Day.

A Word About Maps

The contributors to this volume may have walked fewer miles than one of the early directors of the Ordnance Survey, Major Thomas Colby who, in 1819 walked 586 miles in 22 days, yet they did their bit with a determined spirit. The O.S. map is a boon companion for all travellers on foot and for anyone contemplating all or part of this book's trail then the 1:50,000 scale 'Landranger' series – maps 145, 157, 158, 159, 160, 161, 170, 171 – should get you there, mist or pelting rain permitting.